Technology, Spirituality, & Social Trends

Technology, Spirituality, & Social Trends

PROBING THE HEADLINES
THAT IMPACT YOUR FAMILY

Kerby Anderson
General Editor

kregel
PUBLICATIONS

Grand Rapids, MI 49501

Technology, Spirituality, & Social Trends: Probing the Headlines That Impact Your Family

© 2002 by Probe Ministries

Published by Kregel Publications, a division of Kregel, Inc., P.O. Box 2607, Grand Rapids, MI 49501. Kregel Publications provides trusted, biblical publications for Christian growth and service. Your comments and suggestions are valued.

Unless otherwise indicated, Scripture quotations are from the *New American Standard Bible,* © the Lockman Foundation 1960, 1962, 1963, 1968, 1971, 1972, 1973, 1975, 1977.

Scripture quotations marked NIV are from the *Holy Bible: New International Version®.* © 1973, 1978, 1984 by International Bible Society. Used by permission of Zondervan Publishing House. All rights reserved.

Scripture quotations marked KJV are from the King James version of the Holy Bible.

Scripture quotations marked NKJV are from *The New King James Version.* © 1979, 1980, 1982, Thomas Nelson, Inc., Publishers.

For more information about Kregel Publications, visit our Web site: www.kregel.com.

ISBN 0-8254-2036-9

Printed in the United States of America

1 2 3 4 5 / 06 05 04 03 02

Contents

Foreword

What Shall the Righteous Do?

Y ou'd have to be from another planet not to have noticed that America has radically changed. My father grew up helping his dad farm behind a team of horses. In my children's world, people have walked on the moon and the docking of shuttlecraft at a space station is common fare. By clicking on computer screen icons, they can visit history's most sophisticated library of instant information on anything and everybody. For mere pennies they can bank, buy, sell, and chat immediately with anyone in the world on that invisible highway called the "Web."

Living in America allows us instant access to this "easy street" of fun and games. The latest changes amaze our senses with each new day. In many respects we are blessed to live in such a technologically advanced society. And given the sizzle of it all, one might think that the band is playing the fanfare to announce groundbreaking for the final foundation of Utopia.

Strangely enough, the technological explosion's widgetry has done little to enrich the human spirit. We are more decadent, despairing, and devoid of true fulfillment than ever before. Drugs demonize our youth in the ghetto and on the farm. The most perverse forms of sexual expression are readily accessible by our children. Kids are killing kids. Terrorism has all of us looking over our shoulder.

Hatred and hopelessness have reached a new low when parents strap bombs to the bodies of their young and send them out to destroy themselves with other innocents. The killing of the unborn and the blatant marketing of homosexuality are shrouded in appeals to "choice" and "preference." Poverty and homelessness remain prevalent, and the basic societal infrastructure of the family and education has been eroded under the guise of freedom and personal rights.

Most significantly, in our frenzy to advance ourselves and applaud our achievements, our society has exiled God to the faraway province of irrelevance. And though He is not welcome in our deliberations, He is blamed and despised for oppressively holding the culture back from even more enlightened advancements.

Yet in spite of all that our culture says about how good it is without God, Peter Kreeft is on to something when he observes:

> If we are typically modern . . . we are bored, jaded, cynical, flat, and burnt out. When the skies roll back like a scroll and the angelic trump sounds, many will simply yawn and say, "Pretty good special effects, but the plot's too traditional." If we were not so bored and empty, we would not have to stimulate ourselves with increasing dosages of sex and violence—or just constant busyness. Here we are in the most fantastic fun and games factory ever invented—modern technological society— and we are bored, like a spoiled rich kid in a man-

sion surrounded by a thousand expensive toys. Medieval people by comparison were like peasants in toyless hovels—and they were fascinated. Occasions for awe and wonder seemed to abound: birth and death and love and light and darkness and wind and sea and fire and sunrise and star and tree and bird and human mind—and God and Heaven. But all these things have not changed, we have. The universe has not become empty and we, full; it has remained full and we have become empty, insensitive to its fullness, cold hearted.[1]

I'm reminded of the psalmist's question, "If the foundations are destroyed, What can the righteous do?" (Ps. 11:3). To this point "the righteous" have not done well. Noticing the rapid "slouch toward Gomorrah," we have most often vented anger at activists, politicians, and other purveyors of the decline. Then we crouched in our corners and whined about losing our precious America. With our spirits in a snit, we have often appeared to be just another subgroup with a raised fist demanding our rights and blocking cultural advance.

I fear that we have embarrassed ourselves and our God by appearing to be long on mad and short on mercy.

We should ask ourselves what we expect from a world that refuses to know and listen to the God of the final answer? The real issue is not why our world is not a better place. The more uncomfortable issue is, why are we not more effectively salting our world with the preserving flavor of the reality of Jesus as He is seen in us? And why it is that the "light" of His good works through us is hidden under the bushel of our consternation and confusion (Matt. 5:13–16)?

The sons of Issachar had it right. Among all of King David's men they were applauded because they "understood the times, with knowledge of what Israel should do" (1 Chron. 12:32).

Bravo to my friend Kerby Anderson and his team at Probe Ministries for helping us to understand our times so that we too can know what to do.

—Joseph Stowell

Contributors

Kerby Anderson is the president of Probe Ministries International. He holds a B.S. degree from Oregon State University, an M.F.S. degree from Yale University, and an M.S. degree from Georgetown University. The author of several books, including *Genetic Engineering, Origin Science, Living Ethically in the 90s, Signs of Warning—Signs of Hope,* and *Moral Dilemmas,* Kirby is a nationally syndicated columnist, whose editorials have appeared in the *Dallas Morning News,* the *Miami Herald,* the *San Jose Mercury,* and the *Houston Post.* He is the host of the *Probe* radio program and frequently serves as guest host on *Point of View* (USA Radio Network) and *Open Line* (Moody Broadcasting Network).

Ray Bohlin is the executive director of Probe Ministries. A graduate of the University of Illinois (B.S., zoology), North Texas State University (M.S., population genetics), and the University of Texas at Dallas (M.S., Ph.D., molecular biology), Ray is a co-author of *Natural Limits to Biological Change.* He has also published numerous journal articles. Ray has served as a Research Fellow of the Discovery Institute's Center for the Renewal of Science and Culture.

Sue Bohlin is an associate speaker with Probe. She attended the University of Illinois and Trinity Evangelical Divinity School, and has been a Bible teacher and Christian speaker for more than twenty years. In addition to being a professional calligrapher, she also manages Probe's Web site.

Jerry Solomon served as the field director as well as the coordinator of Mind Games for Probe Ministries until his death in December 2000. Holding a B.A. degree *(summa cum laude)* in Bible and an M.A. degree *(cum laude)* in history and theology from Criswell College, Jerry also attended the University of North Texas, Canal Zone College, and Lebanon Valley College. Jerry worked as a youth pastor and wrote *Sheep Among Wolves*.

Rick Wade is a research associate for Probe Ministries. He holds a B.A. degree in communications (radio broadcasting) from Moody Bible Institute and an M.A. degree *(cum laude)* in Christian thought (theology/philosophy of religion) from Trinity Evangelical Divinity School, where his studies culminated in a thesis on the apologetics of Carl F. H. Henry.

Part 1

Trends in Technology

1

Technological Challenges of the Twenty-first Century

Kerby Anderson

We live in historic times. The twenty-first century presents new challenges, especially in the area of technology. The fields of biotechnology and information technology bode changes to the social landscape, altering the way we make ethical decisions. Because these challenges are not for the fainthearted, we must bring a tough-minded Christianity into the twenty-first century.

First Chronicles 12:32 (NIV) reminds us that the men of Issachar "understood the times and knew what Israel should do." We, too, must understand our times and know what we should do. New ethical challenges await us as we consider the moral issues of our day and analyze them from a biblical perspective.

The task demands humility. More than a hundred years ago, Charles Duell, director of the U.S. Patent Office, was ready to close his office because he believed that everything that can be invented has been invented.[1] Unlike Duell, we should not make the mistake of thinking that we can see into the future. We can, however, analyze trends and new inventions and contemplate their implications. As always, our responsibility is to apply the timeless truths of Scripture to the changing world around us.

How should Christians analyze the technological changes that are taking place? We begin by developing a theology of technology.

Theology of Technology

Technology is nothing more than the modification of the environment to serve human ends. This modification might be a process or activity that extends or enhances a human function. A telescope, for example, extends one's visual perception; a tractor extends one's physical ability; a computer extends one's ability to calculate.

Genesis 1:28 states the biblical mandate for developing and using technology; God gave humankind dominion over the land, and we are obliged to use and manage these resources wisely in serving the Lord. God's ideal was not necessarily a world composed exclusively of primitive areas; before the Fall, Adam was to cultivate and keep the Garden of Eden (Gen. 2:15). After the Fall, the same command pertains to the application of technology to this fallen world, a world that "groans" in travail (Rom. 8:22). Technology can benefit humankind in exercising our proper dominion, and thus remove some of the effects of the Fall (by curing disease, improved breeding livestock, or growing better crops).

Technology is neither good nor evil; rather, its character is determined by the worldview behind the particular technology. In the Old Testament, technology was used for both good (e.g., the building of the ark, Gen. 6) and evil (e.g., the building of the Tower of Babel, Gen. 11). One's focus, therefore, should be not so much on the technology itself but on the philosophical motivation behind its use. Consider the following three important principles.

First, technology is a tool, not as an end in itself. There is nothing sacred about technology. Western culture tends, however, to rely on it more than is appropriate. If, for example, a computer proves a particular point, people tend to accept the computer's conclusion above the well-reasoned conclusion reached by a person. If a machine can do the job, employers are prone to mechanize, even if human labor does the job better or more creatively. Our society often values the work of machines over that done by humans, humans thus becoming servants to machines rather than the other way around.

We look to science and engineering to solve problems that may be the result of human sinfulness (war, prejudice, or greed), the fallen condition of the world (death or disease), or God's curse on Adam (finite resources). In Western culture especially, we tend to believe that technology will save us from our problems. Thus, we use technology as a substitute for God. Christians, though, must not fall into this trap. We must exhibit our ultimate dependence upon God. We must also differentiate between problems that demand a technological solution and ones that can be remedied by a social or spiritual solution.

Second, technology should be appropriately applied. Because humans are created in God's image (Gen. 1:26–27), distinctions exist between humans and animal that call for different applications of medical science. Using artificial insemination to effect genetic improvements in livestock does not justify using the same procedure on human beings. Christians should resist the idea that just because we *can* do something we *should* do it. Technological ability does not equate to moral permission.

Third, ethics, rather than technology, must determine the direction of our society. Jacques Ellul has expressed concern that technology moves society instead of vice versa.[2] Our culture seems all too motivated by a technological imperative that equates the technological ability to do something to a moral imperative to do it. Technology should not, however, determine ethics.

Although scientists might possess the technological ability to be gods, they nevertheless lack the capacity to act like God. Too often, though, humans have used technology for godlike purposes, working out their own physical salvation, enhancing their own development, or even attempting to create life. Christians who take seriously the fallen condition of human beings will readily admit that we often do not know enough about God's creation to wisely use technology. The reality of human sinfulness mandates that great care be taken to prevent the use of technology for greed and exploitation.

Technology's fruits can be both sweet and bitter. C. S. Lewis writes in the *Abolition of Man,* "What we call Man's power over Nature turns out to be power exercised by some men over men with Nature as its instrument. . . . There neither is nor can be any simple increase of power on Man's side. Each new power won *by* man is a power *over* man as well. Each advance leaves him weaker as well as stronger. In every victory, besides being the general who triumphs, he is also the prisoner who follows the triumphal car."[3]

Christians must bring a biblical critique to each technological advance and analyze its impact. Our goal is to liberate the positive effects of technology while restraining its negative effects by setting up appropriate constraints against abuse.

The Challenge of Biotechnology

The age of biotechnology has arrived. For the first time in human history, it is possible to completely redesign existing organisms, including man, and to direct the genetic and reproductive constitution of every living thing. Scientists are no longer limited to crossbreeding and cross-pollinating plants. The tools of biotechnology allow us to change the genetic structure of an organism and bypass the normal processes of reproduction.

Also, for the first time in human history, it is possible to make multiple copies of any existing organism or even certain parts of its genetic structure. This ability to clone existing organisms or their genes gives scientists a tool to reproduce helpful and useful genetic material within a population.

Scientists are also developing techniques to treat and cure genetic diseases through genetic surgery and genetic therapy. Defective genetic sequences have already been identified, and soon scientists will be able to replace these defects with properly functioning genes.

Gene splicing (known as recombinant DNA technology) is fundamentally different from past forms of genetic breeding. Breeding programs work on existing arrays of genetic variability in a species, isolating specific genetic traits through selective breeding. Using gene splicing, scientists can essentially "stack" the deck or even produce an entirely new deck of genetic "cards."

But the ability to change the genetic deck of cards also raises substantial scientific concerns that some "sleight of hand" would produce dangerous consequences. Ethan Singer said, "Those who are powerful in society will do the shuffling; their genes will be shuffled in one direction, while the genes of the rest of us will get shuffled in another."[4] Concern also has been expressed that a reshuffled deck of genes might create an Andromeda strain similar to that envisioned by Michael Crichton in his book by the same title.[5] As in Crichton's book, a microorganism might inadvertently be given the genetic structure of a pathogen for which no antidote or vaccine exists.

The potential benefits of gene splicing, however, are significant. First, the technology can be used to produce medically important substances, among which are insulin, interferon, and human growth hormone. Gene splicing also holds beneficial application in the field of immunology. Currently, to protect organisms from viral disease, doctors must inject a killed or attenuated virus. Scientists using genetic technology can disable a toxin gene, thereby producing a viral substance that triggers production of antibodies without the possibility of producing the disease.

A second benefit of gene splicing can be applied to agriculture through the improved genetic fitness of various plant species. Basic research in gene splicing could lead to efficiency of photosynthesis, increased plant resistance (to salinity, drought, and viruses), and reduction in a plant's demand for nitrogen fertilizer.

Third, gene splicing can aid industrial and environmental processes. Industries that manufacture drugs, plastics, cheese, vitamins, and industrial chemicals will benefit. In regard to the environment, scientists have begun to develop organisms that can clean up oil spills or toxic wastes.

This last benefit also raises one of the greatest scientific concerns over the use of biotechnology. The escape (or even intentional release) of a genetically engineered organism might wreak havoc on the environment. Scientists have created microorganisms that dissolve oil spills or reduce frost on plants. Critics of gene splicing fear that radically altered organisms could occupy new ecological niches, destroy existing ecosystems, driving certain species to extinction.

A significant issue concerns the patenting of these new organisms: Should life-forms be patented at all? Most religious leaders say no. A 1995 gathering of religious leaders who represented virtually every major religious tradition spoke out against the patenting of genetically engineered substances. They argued that life is the creation of God, not humans, and should not be patented as human inventions.[6]

The broader theological question is whether genetic engineering should even be used and, if permitted, *how* it should be used. The natural reaction of many people is to reject new forms of technology for fear they are dangerous. Christians, however, should consider God's command in the cultural mandate (Gen. 1:28). Rather than succumb to the reflex reaction that scientists should not tinker with life, we should instead consider how genetic technology should be used responsibly.

One key issue in relation to responsible use concerns the worldview behind most scientific research. Modern science rests on evolution, assuming that life on this planet is the result of millions of years of a process initiated by chance circumstances. Scientists conclude that intelligent use of science and technology can do a better job than can nature in directing the evolutionary process. Yet even evolutionary scientists warn of the potential danger. Ethan

Singer believes that scientists will "verify a few predictions, and then gradually forget that knowing something isn't the same as knowing everything. . . . At each stage we will get a little cockier, a little surer we know all the possibilities."[7]

In essence, biotechnology gives scientists the tools to drive the evolutionary spiral higher and higher. Julian Huxley looked forward to the day when scientists could fill the "position of business manager for the cosmic process of evolution."[8] That day is coming and in a sense has now arrived. Technology already enables scientists to create new life-forms and alter existing forms of life.

How should Christians respond to this circumstance? We should humbly acknowledge that God is the sovereign Creator and that man has finite knowledge. Genetic technology gives scientists godlike abilities, but all humans lack the wisdom, knowledge, and moral capacity to act like God.

Erwin Chargaff, although the sort of evolutionary scientist who denies the existence of God, nonetheless expresses his concern in regard to genetic tinkering: "Have we the right to counteract, irreversibly, the evolutionary wisdom of millions of years, in order to satisfy the ambition and curiosity of a few scientists?"[9] His answer is no. The Christian's answer should also be the same when we realize that God is the Creator of life. We do not have the right to "rewrite the fifth day of creation."[10]

Does a place exist, however, for genetic engineering within a biblical framework? To answer, consider the distinction between two types of research, the first of which could be called genetic repair. This research attempts to remove genetic defects and develop techniques that will provide treatments for existing diseases. Applications would include various forms of genetic therapy and genetic surgery as well as modifications of existing microorganisms to produce beneficial results.

The Human Genome Project has been able to pinpoint the location and sequence of the approximately 100,000 human genes.[11] Further advances in biotechnology will allow scientists to repair defective sequences, eventually eliminating genetic diseases. Genetic disease is not part of God's plan for the world; it is the result of the Fall (Gen. 3). Christians can approve of applying technology to eliminate these evils, without being accused of fighting against God's will.[12]

A second type of research involves the creation of new forms of life. While Christians may consider it permissible to effect minor modifications of existing organisms, we should be concerned about the large-scale production of new life-forms. The impact on the environment and on humankind could be considerable. Experience has taught what can happen when an existing organism is introduced into a new environment (e.g., the rabbit into Australia, the rat into Hawaii, or the gypsy moth into the United States). One can only imagine the devastation that might occur when a newly created organism is introduced into a new environment.

God created plants and animals as "kinds" (Gen. 1:24). Although minor variability exists within these created kinds, built-in barriers exist between them. The result of redesigning creatures of any kind cannot be predicted in the same way that properties can be predicted for new elements on the periodic chart. Recombinant DNA technology offers great promise in treating genetic disease, but Christians should nonetheless practice vigilance. Although this technology is a boon for repairing genetic defects, it should not be used to confer on scientists the role of creator.

A related issue in the field of biotechnology is that of human cloning. Many nonhuman mammals have already been cloned, and it has become apparent that the cloning of a human being will no doubt take place at some time in the future. Proponents of human cloning argue that doing so is a worthwhile endeavor for at least three reasons. First, cloning could be used to produce spare parts. A cloned kidney, for example, would be genetically identical to the original person, thus that person's immune system would not reject the cloned organ as readily as it would reject a donated organ. Second, proponents argue that cloning might be a way to replace a lost child. A dying infant or child could be cloned so that a couple could replace the child with a genetically identical child. Third, cloning could produce biological immortality. One woman approached scientists to clone her deceased father and even offered to carry the cloned baby to term.[13]

While cloning of various organisms may be permissible, cloning a human being raises significant questions, the first of which concerns the sanctity of life. Human beings are created in the image of God (Gen. 1:27–28) and therefore differ from animals. Human cloning would certainly threaten the sanctity of human life at numerous levels. First, as shown with the first cloned sheep, cloning is an inefficient process of procreation. Second, cloning would no doubt produce genetic accidents. Earlier experiments with frogs produced numerous embryos that did not survive, and many of those that did survive developed into grotesque monsters. Third, cloning raises concerns for pro-life proponents. Researchers often clone human embryos for various experiments. Although the

National Bioethics Advisory Commission banned cloning of human beings, it permitted the cloning of human embryos for research. Because these embryos are ultimately destroyed, the research raises the same pro-life concerns as does abortion.

Cloning represents a tampering with the reproductive process at the most basic level. Cloning a human being certainly strays substantially from God's intended procedure of a man and woman producing children within the bounds of matrimony (Gen. 2:24). All sorts of bizarre scenarios can be envisioned. Some homosexual advocates argue that cloning would be an ideal way for homosexual men to reproduce themselves.

Although human cloning could be an alternative form of reproduction, one wonders if human clones would be fully human. Too, because cloning is a drastic diversion from God's intended process of procreation, some people wonder if a clone would have a soul. A traducian view of the origin of the soul believes that a person receives both body and soul from his or her parents rather than from God. Thus, purports this view, a cloned human being would have a soul and would in a sense be no different than an identical twin.

It is conceivable, in fact, for genetic engineering to produce innumerable copies of the same person. James Bonner says that "there is nothing to prevent us from taking a thousand [cells]. We could grow any desired number of genetically identical people from individuals who have desirable characteristics."[14] Such a vision conjures images of Alphas, Betas, Gammas, and Deltas from Aldous Huxley's book *Brave New World* and provides a dismal contrast to God's creating each human as a unique individual.

As such, each person contributes to both the unity and the diversity of humanity. The Jewish Midrash expresses this position well: "For a man stamps many coins in one mold and they are all alike; but the King who is king over all kings, the Holy One blessed be he, stamped every man in the mold of the first man, yet not one of them resembles his fellow."[15] A Christian position, then, would reject future research toward cloning a human being and would reject as well cloning as an alternative means of reproduction.

The Challenge of Information Technology

The information revolution constitutes a technological advance the potential of which holds great promise for all persons but raises concerns for Christians. The shift to using computers has been both swift and spectacular. The first electronic digital computer, ENIAC, weighed thirty tons, contained eighteen thousand vacuum tubes, and occupied a space as large as a boxcar.[16] Less than forty years later, handheld calculators had comparable computing power and cost only a few dollars. Today's desktop computers possess more computing power than engineers could imagine even a few years ago.

The impact of computers on our society was probably best illustrated when in 1982 *Time* magazine picked the computer as its "Man of the Year"—actually listing it as "Machine of the Year."[17] In contrast, it is hard to imagine a picture of the Spirit of St. Louis or an Apollo lunar excursion module featured in a magazine as "Machine of the Year."

As spectacular as has been the increase in computer use, so has been the shift to an information-based society. In a sense, the computer age and the information age go hand in hand and, indeed, the computer is helpful in managing information, which is expanding exponentially. The information stored in the world's libraries and computers doubles every eight years.[18]

But the rapid development and deployment of computing power has raised significant social and moral questions. Often, though, people ignore the questions or become confused by them.

One key concern is computer crime, which is merely a new spin on old crimes such as fraud, larceny, and embezzlement. Those crimes are, however, carried out through more sophisticated means.

Computer fraud often arises from the centralization of information, which gives computer criminals, or hackers, access to addresses, records, and files. Governmental agencies, banks, and businesses use computers to collect information on its citizens and customers. The federal government, for example, has an estimated fifteen files on each American.[19] Nothing is inherently wrong with collecting information, if it can be kept confidential and is not used for immoral actions. Confidentiality, however, is often difficult to guarantee.

The centralization of information in an information-based society can be as dangerous, given sinful man in a fallen world, as the centralization of power. In the past, centralized information processing was used for persecution. When Adolf Hitler's Gestapo began rounding up millions of Jews, information about their religious affiliation was stored in shoe boxes. At the beginning of World War II, U.S. Census Bureau punch cards were used to round up Japanese Americans living on the West Coast.[20] Modern technology makes such tasks that much easier. Governmental agencies routinely collect information about citizens' ethnic origin, race, religion, gross income, and even political associations.

Moreover, the problem is not limited to governmental agencies. Many banking systems, for example, use electronic funds-transfer systems. Plans to link these systems together into a national system could also provide a means of tracking the actions of citizens. A centralized banking network could fulfill nearly every information need that a malevolent dictator might imagine. This is not to say that such evils will occur, but societies that want to monitor their citizens will, with computer technology, be able to do so more efficiently.

A problem related to centralized computer information concerns the confidentiality of computer records. Records kept by computer can be mishandled or abused the same as those of any other system. Reputations built up over a lifetime can be ruined by computer errors, and often the victim has little recourse. At present, only one piece of legislation addresses confidentiality: the 1974 Privacy Act allows citizens to find out what records federal bureaucracies have on them and to correct any errors.[21]

The proliferation of computers presents yet another set of social and moral concerns. In the recent past, most centralized information required an expertise in FORTRAN—a computer language—to access it. Now, because of personal computers and the Internet, most people have access to information that was formerly very difficult to obtain. This easy access to information, plus computers that have the capability to tie into other computers, provides more opportunities for computer crime.

The news media frequently carry reports about hackers who have been able to gain access to confidential computer systems and obtain or interfere with the data banks.

Although such data banks are supposed to be secure, enterprising hackers break in anyway. In many cases, such security breaches involved merely curious teenagers. Nevertheless, computer hacking has become a developing area of crime. Criminals might use computer access to forge documents, change records, and draft checks. They can even use computers for blackmail by holding files for ransom and threatening to destroy them if their demands are not met. Unless better methods of security are found, professional criminals will begin to crack computer security codes and gain quick access into sensitive files.

As happens with most technological breakthroughs, the engineers have outpaced the lawmakers. Computer deployment has created a number of legal questions. First is the problem of establishing penalties for computer crimes. Typically, centralized computer information and intellectual property has a different status than does real or personal property in our criminal justice system. Currently the notion exists that ideas and information are not afforded the same legal status as, say, an automobile or jewelry. Legislation is needed that will deter criminals, or even curious hackers, from breaking into confidential records or from using the computer to steal patented or copyrighted property.

A second legal problem arises from the question of jurisdiction. Telecommunications allows information to be shared across state and even national borders. Few federal statutes govern this practice, and less than half of the states have laws dealing with information abuse.

Enforcement is also be a problem for several reasons, one of which is, as stated above, the problem of jurisdiction. Computers are, after all, nearly as ubiquitous as telephones or photocopiers. A second reason is that police departments rarely train their personnel in computer abuse and fraud. A third reason is lack of personnel as well as lack of funds for hiring extra personnel to deal with computer crime.

Computer fraud also raises questions about the role of insurance companies. How do companies insure an electronic asset? What value does computer information have? These questions will inevitably need to be addressed.

Technology and Human Nature

These new technologies challenge our views of human nature. Already, medical technology challenges our views of what it means to be human. As stated earlier, the key issue in embryonic research, as in the abortion debate, is when does human life begin? Is an embryo human? What about a developing fetus? Although the Bible provides answers to these questions, society often takes its cue from pronouncements that do not square with biblical truth.

Biotechnology raises a further set of questions. Is a frozen embryo human and deserving of a right to life? Is a clone human? Would a clone have a soul? These questions and more will add fuel to the debate. Although the Bible doesn't address directly such issues as genetically engineered humans or clones, key biblical passages (e.g., Pss. 51:5; 139) seem to teach that an embryo is a human created in the image of God.

Information technology also raises questions about human nature in an unexpected way. Researchers believe that as computer technology advances, we will begin to analyze the human mind in physical terms. In *The Society of Mind,* Marvin Minsky, professor at the Massachusetts Institute of Technology, says that "the mind, the soul, the self, are not a single ghostly entity but a society of agents, deeply integrated, yet each one rather mindless on its own."[22] He dreams of being able to ultimately reduce mind (and therefore human nature) to natural mechanisms. Obviously, this dream is not based upon empirical evidence but nonetheless attempts to reduce everything (including mind) to matter.

If Professor Minsky's dream of reducing the essence of humanness to mere matter becomes accepted as reality, will we someday elevate computers to the level of humanity? An article asks, "Would an Intelligent Computer Have a 'Right to Life'?"[23] Computer rights might be something that society would consider; many people are already willing to grant certain rights to animals.

In a sense, the question of computer rights is whether an intelligent computer would have a soul and therefore access to fundamental human rights. As bizarre as the question might sound, it is no doubt inevitable. When seventeenth-century philosopher Gottfried Wilhelm von Leibniz first described a thinking machine, he was careful to point out that this machine would not have a soul—fearful perhaps of reaction from the church.[24] Already, scientists predict that computer intelligence will create "an intelligence beyond man's" and provide wonderful new capabilities.[25] One of the great challenges in the future will be how to manage new computing power that will outstrip human intelligence.

Once again, technology creates challenges for Christians in the twenty-first century. Human beings are more than just proteins and nucleic acids. Human beings are more than bits and bytes. We are created in the image of God and therefore have a spiritual dimension. Perhaps this point must be our central message to a world enamored of technology: Human beings are created in the image of God and must be treated with dignity and respect.

2

The Value of the Internet for Christians

Sue Bohlin

The Internet is a cultural force that is changing the way we live and communicate. But many people don't understand it. This chapter examines the Internet as a tool for Christians to use to the glory of God while simultaneously practicing discernment in its use.

An Exciting Technology

The Internet is like a system of highways, but the Net includes both the roadways and the destinations. Just as you can travel in a car over a series of connected interstates, state highways, city streets, farm-to-market roads, and gravel lanes, you can travel the Internet electronically through a network of computers that allows you to get just about anywhere in moments. The destinations in your electronic travels are much like different kinds of malls, where the stores are all situated next to each other. News and entertainment malls offer everything from fine art in the Louvre (www.louvre.fr) to breaking news stories,[1] video clips of live performances, speeches,[2] music,[3] and radio stations on the other side of the globe (www.radio-stations.net). Information malls let you research and gather information on everything from Caribbean vacations to the Crusades to castles.[4] Library malls offer, instead of books, files of everything from games to computer software to historical documents.[5] And conversation malls let you talk to people across town or around the world.[6]

The Internet also provides almost instantaneous electronic mail, or e-mail, which allows people to communicate so quickly, easily, and cheaply that e-mails now outnumber physical mail, aptly nicknamed "snail mail." You don't have to track down paper and pen, handwrite the note or letter (and these days, legible handwriting is becoming all too rare), find a stamp, and then walk it to a mailbox. Instead, you type in a letter at a keyboard, type in an e-mail address, hit the "send" button, and bam! Your letter is in the other person's mailbox waiting for them to log on and read it.

You can also subscribe to electronic, automated mailing lists, which are a blend of newsletter and discussion group devoted to a single, specialized topic. My friend Bill, whose eight-year-old daughter, Cheska, lost her battle with cancer, was grateful for the Brain Tumor list.[7] Subscribers to this list are patients with brain tumors, families or friends of brain-tumor patients, and health-care professionals who treat brain-tumor patients or do research on brain tumors. Bill gleaned valuable information about and leads on research and therapies. He also gave and received support and encouragement through a community of people bound by a common tragic bond.

The instant, easy communication of e-mail also made it possible for Cheska to receive prayer support from literally around the world. By sending prayer updates to more than two hundred people, her father discovered that, by word of mouth and computer, thousands of people all over the globe prayed for her. I discovered the same kind of response. When I sent requests for prayers and cards for my father to the barbershop (singing) community during his battle with cancer, he was delighted to receive encouragement from all sorts of people whom he didn't know.

The Internet is one of the most exciting developments that the world has seen. Yet many Christians are both fearful and ignorant of it. We don't have to be. Like any other technology, the Internet is morally neutral. How we use it or abuse it makes it either good or evil.

Home Schoolers and Missionaries

The Internet has been a tremendous boon to families. The Internet's rich informational resources provide a way to share common interests. One father and his son like to surf the World Wide Web to explore their mutual passions for the Civil War and astronomy.[8] Another father-son duo used the Internet to decide which historical places they would visit while planning a battlefield tour. Many families have enjoyed researching their vacation destinations before leaving home. In our family, we used the Internet to learn as much as we could about Costa Rica before our son headed there on a missions trip. Our other son researched the artist M. C. Escher for a paper in school and found biographical information and examples of his artwork on the World Wide Web. His search yielded relevant and in-depth information—and saved us a trip to the library!

Home-school families have also discovered the benefits of the Internet. Information available online can supplement lessons and provide resources for the parent-teacher. Online encyclopedias,[9] newspapers, and libraries[10] offer more information to home schoolers than has ever been available before. But beyond information, Internet mailing lists, as well as forums accessed through online services such as CompuServe and America Online, offer the support and interaction home schoolers can enjoy with other home schoolers. Families in the most remote corners of Canada can enjoy an electronic camaraderie with similar families in suburban Atlanta and even military families in Germany. They can share insights and experiences with each other and brainstorm together on problems, and on challenges such as finding a way to teach a child a certain concept or how to address the requirements of a special needs child. "Plugged-in" home-school families report that the encouragement of their online home-school communities is often what keeps them going.

As computer video capabilities become cheaper and more accessible, home-school families look forward to networking with others during learning exercises. A family's geographical location makes no difference in a virtual (electronic) classroom.

The Internet is also a huge blessing for missionaries and mission organizations. Radio and satellite links give missionaries in even the most remote outposts access to instant, inexpensive, reliable communication via e-mail with their organizations and families. The Internet has shrunk the world, and missionaries no longer have to feel isolated. One missionary in the former Soviet Union told me, via e-mail, that she was very grateful for almost instant access to both loved ones and mature, wise believers who can encourage and guide her as she deals with the challenges of missions work. But the best thing, she said,

was that she can ask people to pray specifically and immediately for needs and problems and see responses within
hours instead of weeks or months. A missionary who is
battling discouragement, homesickness, and weakness, not
to mention the intensity of spiritual warfare, can summon
real-time prayer assistance from the other side of the world
and can experience real support and a sense of being connected to the larger body of Christ.

Whether a parent is saying good-bye to a child who is
headed for the mission field, a foreign military post, or
even to college in another part of the state, the Internet
makes it easier for them to part. They can stay in close
contact with their loved ones in a world that has grown
smaller as the Internet has grown larger.

Dangers on the Internet

Although the Internet provides a wealth of information, not all of it is edifying or wise. Much of it is down-
right silly, and some of it is actually dangerous. You don't,
of course, have to worry that when you turn on your computer a pornographic picture will fall into your lap. Porn
pushers are, however, becoming increasingly aggressive
in finding ways to send their pictures to unsuspecting
people, often children.

The key to protecting our children from online pornography is the same way we protect them from printed
pornography: parental vigilance. Parents need to know
what their children are doing at the computer, so it's wise
to keep the family computer in a central location. And it's
also wise for parents themselves to become computer and
Internet literate. Powerful tools exist to help parents and
schools keep adult-oriented material away from children.
Software programs filter objectionable sites and prevent

access to them. The Dallas Association for Decency (DAD, www.4decency.com) evaluates Internet filters that examine the four sources of pornography: Web pages, which are like magazine articles replete with pictures; Usenet newsgroups, a series of messages and discussions upon which people post pictures and text (and the Internet's most egregious source of porn); Internet Relay Chat (IRC) channels, electronic chat rooms where people can talk without any monitoring; and File Transfer Protocol (FTP) sites, which are like library stacks consisting of nothing but files for the taking. Several Internet service providers (ISPs) offer filtered service, maintaining the filter on a remote computer. This is the safest and most effective system because it is much harder for technically savvy kids to circumvent than is a filtering program that you install on your own computer. One top-rated and well-respected filtered ISP is ViaFamily (www.viafamily.com).

But some families don't want dial-up Internet service, which is much slower than broadband (fast, cable, or DSL) Internet. In that case, the next best thing is a filter on your computer. The two best, in DAD's opinion, are FamilyClick (www.familyclick.com) and N2H2 (www.n2h2.com). Just having a filtering program isn't enough, however. Not all filtering software is created equal, and some programs work so poorly that they're actually worse than nothing at all, because they give a false sense of security. Nothing takes the place of parental involvement and vigilance—the first line of defense!

But what about when our kids are at school? Administrators, although they want to provide access to Internet resources, are very much aware of online dangers. Many school districts are in the process of developing Acceptable Use Policies that will provide stringent parameters for student Internet access. It's essential that parents check on the policies of their children's schools. Parents, too, should check the policy at their local public libraries, which, out of a misguided allegiance to noncensorship, often provide unfiltered access to both adults and children.

A danger of a very different kind also requires our vigilance. Computer viruses float around on the Internet. They are transmitted when a file is transferred from a remote computer to your own (downloading) or from an infected diskette to a clean one. A virus is an invisible program that is written by programmers, who range from mischievous to mean-spirited, and that attaches itself to a file, wreaking some degree of havoc on an unsuspecting person's computer. It's important to use virus detecting software that scans your hard disk and diskettes for viruses and then destroys them. I used to be less vigilant about checking my computer for viruses, and on March 6—the birthday of Michelangelo—the virus of the same name wiped out all of my data—and the data of a few thousand other computers as well. A little caution goes a long way. Be sure to use—and update—virus protection software by companies such as Norton or McAfee.

Online Communication

Ann Landers and Abigail Van Buren each write an advice column. Both feature an increasing number of letters about spouses who emotionally or physically abandoned their families after meeting people through the computer. Those who have never developed a relationship with someone who lives on the other side of a screen and a telephone line have a hard time understanding how such a thing could happen. The immediacy of computer communication offers an electric thrill, as if a radio personality suddenly started conversing with you through your radio.

The dynamics of computer conversation are vastly different than face-to-face discussion. Computer conversation includes no nonverbal element, which comprises 93 percent of our communication. When body language and tone of voice are missing, and words are the only medium, words become much more important. And words, especially those of a direct and personal nature, are very powerful. But, under the right circumstances, words on a screen are enough to allow friendships to sprout up quickly and mature. Many people count their online friends, some of whom they've never met, as among their most cherished relationships. And many Christians are grateful for the depth of fellowship with other believers that they have found through the computer.

It's important to understand, however, how online relationships differ from those in the "real world." Because we have limited information about the people with whom we communicate online, we unconsciously project our preconceptions and fantasies onto them. Real life can be ordinary and drab compared to the idealized image we relate to on the screen. One person finally realized the reason she preferred her online friends to her real-life relationships; as she put it, she "had imbued them with magic."

It's not surprising, then, that emotional potholes exist in cyberspace. Through shared words, thoughts, and feelings one easily achieves a false sense of emotional intimacy. Missing, however, is the fullness of another person's whole personality and the context of his or her three-dimensional life. What people experience through online contact is generally not true intimacy, although a relationship can indeed be extremely intense, and most people are unprepared for the level of intensity that can characterize online communication. Sometimes, though, that experience of emotional intimacy can come at the cost of intimacy in one's real-life relationships. Many husbands and wives feel shut out of their spouse's heart and mind because he or she spends hours a day at the computer, communing with unseen people with whom they readily share their deepest selves.

Women are especially vulnerable in online communication for two reasons. First, God made us verbal creatures, and we respond deeply to words. And words are everything in cyberspace. Second, women are vulnerable because of the pervasive loneliness in our culture. Even women in marriages and families experience unmet needs for attention, warmth, and interaction. Many women are starving for romance, and any attention from a man seems like food for their famished romantic spirits. When a woman receives focused attention from a man who is listening to not only her heart but also her words, the experience can feel to her like the romance that God designed her to receive. Thus, a frightening number of women, although it happens to men as well, become infatuated with a person of the opposite sex whom they've never even seen. The Word of God tells us to guard our hearts (Prov. 4:23)—wise advice for all online communications and relationships.

Christian Resources

Never before has accessing so many Christian ministries and their material been so easy. It's now possible for us at Probe Ministries to make our radio transcripts available, without printing or mailing costs, to anyone in the world who has Internet access. And Internet surfers can, by using search engines[11] (programs that scour the net for anything they can find on a given subject) stumble across biblically based, Christian perspectives without even meaning to. Someone looking for information on angels, for example, will find Probe's essay[12] alongside articles from a typically New Age perspective. Several Web sites offer links to many Christian ministries. Gospel Communications Network (www.gospelcom.net) is the home for InterVarsity (www.gospelcom.net/iv), Navigators (www.gospelcom.net/navs), and Radio Bible Class (www.gospelcom.net/rbc), where you can now read the well-known devotional *Our Daily Bread* (www.gospelcom.net/rbc/odb) online.

If you have a computer, a modem, and an Internet provider, you have access to literature and reference works beyond the scope of many libraries. One favorite Internet site is the Institute for Christian Leadership's amazing "Guide to Christian Literature on the Net."[13] There you can browse various Bibles, articles, classic essays, creeds and confessions, sermons, and reference works. They also offer the "Guide to Early Church Documents on the Net,"[14] a real find for church history buffs.

Wheaton College sponsors the "Christian Classics Ethereal Library" (www.ccel.org), offering writings by saints such as Thomas Aquinas, Augustine, John Calvin, and Jonathan Edwards. Their collection of reference works is thrilling to Bible students. There you can find a concordance, a Bible dictionary, a topical Bible, and Matthew Henry's commentary. One of the best Christian resources is the Bible Gateway (bible.gospelcom.net), where you can locate any chapter or verse in the most popular English versions, as well as Spanish, German, French, Swedish, Tagalog, and Latin! If you're a teacher or a pastor, check out the Blue Letter Bible (www.blueletterbible.org) for wonderful study tools.

But the Internet doesn't limit itself to only what can be seen. With software such as Internet Explorer or Netscape—that comes as part of Web browsers—or by downloading the free software program RealAudio (www.real.com), it's possible to listen to a variety of audio clips. You can hear a sermon by Chuck Swindoll (www.insight.org) or David Jeremiah (www.turningpt.org). You can enjoy various kinds of music and radio stations such as those discussed earlier.

A lot of information is available to Christians on the Internet. Want to find a Christian radio station near you or in a city that you'll be visiting? The Web site www.christianradio.com lists hundreds of them. You can find Christian clipart on the Internet (timoart.com) and even download hymns and worship music to play through your computer's sound card.[15]

If you want to stay current on new Christian sites, there's great news. Quentin Schultze has revised his book *Internet for Christians*,[16] as well as a Web site by the same name. The site features a continually updated "virtual appendix" to the book (www.gospelcom.net/ifc). Dr. Schultze also offers on the Web site the "Internet for Christians Newsletter," which is e-mailed free biweekly. I also recommend Jason Baker's excellent resource, *Parents' Computer Companion.*[17]

Happy surfing!

Protecting Your Family on the Internet

Sue Bohlin

I t is not just airbrushed naked women anymore. Available for free on the Internet—and sometimes delivered without our asking—are pictures of people actually engaging in various types of sex, bestiality, and molestation of children by adults.

Protecting from Pornography

Like the tobacco industry once did, the pornography industry aggressively targets young children as consumers. Pornographers position their Web sites to be found in innocent searches that use words such as *toys*, *Disney*, *Nintendo*, or *dolls*. According to NetValue, in September 2000, children spent 64.9 percent more time on pornography sites than they did on game sites. One-quarter (27.5 percent) of American children, age seventeen and under, visited adult Web sites, a statistic that represents three million underage visitors.[1]

But children are not the only ones lured by easy and

anonymous access to pornography; more than two hundred thousand Americans, classified as "cybersex compulsives," are addicted to e-porn. A study, conducted by psychologists at Stanford and Duquesne universities, appears in the March 2001 issue of the journal *Sexual Addiction and Compulsivity.* And as of this writing, some people with whom I am acquainted are now in jail for stealing to support their porn addiction. Pastors hear from scores of people in their congregations who are secretly addicted to cyberporn. Exposure to pornography for some people escalates into more perverse and dehumanizing images. Online pornography is so strongly graphic that it can send a hormonal power surge through the brain that has been called "electronic crack cocaine."

Preventing online pornography from reaching our homes and our children, then, is a serious and legitimate concern. Parental involvement is the first line of defense, and Internet filters will add an additional layer of security in the home. Whether the device used is a filtered Internet service provider, a filtering software program, or even hardware filters, which just recently became available, some level of filtering is better than none, but no such device is perfect. The technology is developing every day, however, and filters today are far more effective and less intrusive than they were only a couple of years ago.

Many organizations have tested filtering technologies, and their evaluations and experience is available to parents. The Center for Decency (www.centerfordecency.org), the National Coalition for the Protection of Children and Families (www.filterreview.org), and a combination of several organizations at www.getnetwise.org are excellent resources. Those sites will provide not only advice to parents about monitoring their children's or spouse's online activities but also resources to deal with situations that arise if pornography is already a problem in the home.

Protecting our families from Internet pornography in our homes, businesses, schools, and libraries is one of the most loving and important things we can do for them. Put your computer in a central location in your home where anyone can see what's on the screen. Determine how much time children can spend online. Some families link screen time to reading time: a half hour of reading earns you thirty minutes of Internet time. Talk to your children about the dangers of pornography. We warned our boys about "mind dirt," the kind of mental images that, like the mud that was ground into their soccer uniforms, can't be washed out of memory. Talk about why pornography is wrong: it destroys the dignity that God gives people, who are made in His image, and it fuels our flesh instead of our spirits.[2]

Protecting from Predators

Several years ago when my son was about eight or nine, we had a memorable conversation when he decided to run away from home. I used all of the arguments from reason, trying to dissuade him, but he was determined to leave. He was quite confident that if he met any bad guys, he'd just "beat 'em up," and that would be the end of that. I had to tell him about the *real* bad guys who look for vulnerable runaways, alone and defenseless, and who either capture or lure them to places where they make horrible videos of grown-ups doing horrible things to kids. My son decided to stay home.

As parents we want, of course, to protect our kids from predators "out there" in the world, but it's just as important to protect them from predators online. Evil people and pedophiles know how to find children who haven't yet learned to be suspicious and self-protective, and the bad guys often rationalize their actions by saying, "If parents don't protect their kids, then they deserve whatever happens."

One of the least safe places on the Internet is chat rooms. Conversations start out in a group, but one person can invite another into a private conversation, called an "instant message," or IM. Teach your kids not to go into chat rooms or have private conversations unless you are supervising their activity. Some "kids" they meet in chat rooms or IMs might not be kids at all but adults with bad intentions.

Set down safety rules for your family. Teach your kids never to give out personal information such as their age, phone number, school, or your town or city. Don't even let them use their real names. Kids must never call or meet an online friend in person unless a parent is there. And it would be wise not to have a personal profile, which is a big part of not only the America Online community but also Web sites such as Yahoo. Predators prowl the profiles looking for likely victims.

Donna Rice Hughes,[3] a children's Internet safety advocate, suggests some questions to ask your kids who spend time online:

- Have you seen any pornographic pictures?
- Has anyone online talked dirty to you?
- Have you met anyone online whom you don't know?
- Has anyone asked you for personal information?
- Has anyone asked to meet you in person?

Ask the questions, and watch your kids' body language for clues that anything has happened. We must remain on the alert in order protect our kids from predators.

Protecting Ourselves Emotionally

The Internet has opened a virtual Pandora's box of emotional disasters for huge numbers of people. An innocent-looking computer screen or television set (for those with WebTV) turns out to be a portal to enormously addictive and powerful relationships with people we would never otherwise meet. A person can be overwhelmed by the sense of truly connecting with another person in an intense, compelling way. It can be a shock and a thrill to get a computer for doing the mundane tasks of word processing or bookkeeping, and then discover that when the computer connects to the Internet live people are on the other side of the screen.

The nature of online communication is different from the face-to-face or telephone communication we're used to in real life (or RL, in net-speak). For one thing, people can project themselves as they *wish* to be rather than as they really are. The painfully shy introvert can become a witty conversationalist, the charismatic center of attention in a chat room. Overweight, slovenly people can pretend to be buff and beautiful. Middle-aged men can—and do—present themselves as young girls.

Online communication, then, often isn't between *people* as much as between *personas.* Add to that the development of a rapid sense of intimacy, and you have the potential for people to get hurt by not guarding their hearts (see Prov. 4:23). One young man, for instance, met disaster when, lonely after his divorce, he thought that he fell in love with a young lady he met in a chat room. They started talking by phone. He professed his love for her, she professed her love for him. She visited him for a romantic weekend tryst. But it turned out that she was a fourteen-year-old runaway, not eighteen as she had said, and when her parents tracked her down they had him arrested as a sex offender.[4]

Many married people have discovered how intrusive the Internet can be when their spouses spend hours online in chat rooms and in private conversations. Many marriages have broken up over online affairs. It doesn't matter whether the relationships become physical; when people give their affections to another person, it's adultery of the heart.

How do we protect ourselves emotionally?

First, predecide to guard your heart. If you start to think about someone in a way that would embarrass you if others knew, pull back. You're probably spending too much time online and spending too much emotional energy on that person. Redirect your thoughts to things that are more righteous.

Second, if you're married, shore up your relationship. Spend at least as much time building your marriage as you spend with online friends. Resolve not to take your spouse for granted or compare him or her to your image of your online friends. Remember that we tend to project onto online friends the qualities we want them to have. It's not fair to compare the reality of the person to whom you're married with the fantasy of the persona on the other side of the screen. Consider that it is extremely rare—and, frankly, unwise—for married people to have close friends of the opposite sex.

Third, watch how much of your heart you share with people online. They are, after all, strangers. Our emotions follow our hearts, and when we give pieces of our hearts away by sharing our hopes and dreams and feelings, our affections are also tied to those pieces. Such heart sharing has been called "emotional fornication," and with good reason.

Realize how quickly and easily one can fall into the false and fast intimacy of online relationships. Remember, the intimacy is not real, but the pain might be.

Protecting Ourselves Financially

Every year, more and more people are buying and selling on the Internet. The proliferation of e-commerce means more opportunity for fraud, mischief, and flat-out evil intentions. We need to be good stewards of God's money online, just as we are every other place. So how do we protect ourselves financially?[5]

First, protect your online identity. Identity theft is a growing problem, and the Internet has only made it easier. Don't store your personal information or credit card numbers with online retailers. Reputable merchants will ask if you want them to keep track of your personal information so you don't have to enter it every time. It's not that hard or time-consuming for you to keep your own information, and it's a good way to protect yourself. Don't give out more information than is necessary, especially your Social Security number. You're not being paranoid when you refuse to do so; you're being wise.

Next, you don't have to be afraid to make a purchase online if you do business with a reputable company or organization. To ensure, however, that you're dealing with a real company or organization, look for a physical address and at least one customer service number (Call to make sure that it's active.). Check out the company online at the Better Business Bureau (www.bbb.org).

Before entering personal information, only use a secure, or encrypted, connection. Look at the site's Web address. If it changed to "https," the *s* shows that it's secure. But not all secure connections use the https designation. Regardless, you absolutely *must* see that the padlock icon on your Web browser is locked.

Once you place your order, print a copy of your online order and keep it for the length of the return or warranty period. Your printed copy might be the only proof of your purchase.

Use a credit card instead of a debit card. Credit cards give you bargaining leverage if you need to dispute a charge—if, for instance, the item never arrived. Using a debit card, however, is like spending cash; once the money is out of your account, it's gone.

If you participate in online auctions such as eBay or Amazon.com, be aware that auctions are the number one online scam today.[6] To ensure you get what you bid for, use a third-party escrow service whereby the seller doesn't get paid until the buyer receives and approves the purchase. Most money lost in Internet scamming is through the Nigerian money offers. "These offers, which used to come by airmail but now are increasingly arriving by e-mail, promise millions of dollars in exchange for allowing your bank account to be used to safeguard someone else's riches. But the real intent is to take money out of your account, not put money in it."[7]

Protecting Ourselves from Loss

The rise of the Internet has opened new doors to loss, from which the wise person protects himself or herself. Probably the biggest loss is time, and probably the biggest time-waster is chat rooms. They are not productive, and many of them, as has been discussed, are not safe. Chat rooms are a way to spend time, but they encourage a false sense of intimacy and community. When we stand before the judgment seat of Christ, one wonders how much of that chat room activity will withstand the fiery test and endure into eternity (see 1 Cor. 3:12–15).

Another consumer of time is e-mail. E-mail is, like hand-written letters, often valuable for true communication and, like newspapers, is often valuable for disseminating infor-mation. But a lot of time is spent forwarding messages that are actually urban legends and hoaxes. Don't waste your time or anybody else's by passing on e-mails that promise goodies in exchange for forwarding the message to a certain number of people. No such thing as e-mail tracking exists. Nobody will know if you forwarded the message, and you won't ever get the goodies.

Consider, too, fake virus warnings. I get several a week (often per day) that urge me to forward the warning to everyone in my address book. Before you pass on a virus warning, check it out at sites such as Vmyths.com that expose virus warning hoaxes.

But real viruses are a true threat, and they can wipe out data on your computer. Such losses can be avoided by us-ing virus-protection, including Norton Anti-Virus and McAfee VirusScan. Don't open e-mail attachments if you don't know either what they are or the person who sent them. (The e-mail message itself is not a danger. It's the attachments you need to be concerned about.) Many pro-grams can infect your computer and send out copies of themselves to people in your address book, and you won't even know it's happening. Because I send Probe Minis-tries' online newsletter, the *Probe-Alert*, I regularly receive replies containing viruses and worms from people I don't know. Their infected e-mail programs send a nasty sur-prise for my computer.

This chapter has considered ways to protect ourselves and our families from online pornography and online predators. Suggested, too, were ways to prevent emotional and financial disasters as well as losses of time and data. It is hoped that something has been passed along that will help you pursue the worthy scriptural goal of "do[ing] all to the glory of God" (1 Cor. 10:31)—even in your online life.

4

Cyberporn

Kerby Anderson

Pornography is coming to a computer screen near you. The combination of sex and the computer was inevitable, but the raunchiness of what can be viewed has shocked even the jaded.

The electronic revolution has made pornography more accessible, bringing decadent and hard-to-get images into the home. In the past, those who wanted to obtain hardcore pornography had to leave their home and go to a seedy side of town and buy a magazine or watch a movie. That is no longer the case. First came cable TV, broadcasting sexual images that were more explicit than those seen in movie theaters two decades before. Then came videos, which could be rented at your local respectable video store.

But the expansion of computer databases on the Internet has provided to both adults and children the greatest access yet to sexually explicit images. Images that used to come through the mail in a plain brown wrapper can now be obtained and viewed in the privacy of one's home.

Parents especially have a legitimate concern about what their children will be exposed to and the damage that it can do. One ten-year-old student spent time talking to other kids by computer in the Treehouse chat room on America Online. One day, he received an e-mail from a stranger, and it contained a mysterious file with instructions on how to download it. He followed the instructions and then called his mom. When his mom opened the file, the computer screen filled with thumbnail-size images of "couples engaged in various acts of sodomy, heterosexual intercourse and lesbian sex."[1]

Parents need also be concerned about their children being lured by a sexual predator. Los Angeles Detective Bill Dworn warns, "The pervert can get on any bulletin board and chat with kids all night long. He lies about his age and makes friends. As soon as he can get a telephone number or address, he's likely to look up the kid and molest him or her."[2]

Those who object to any infringement whatsoever upon First Amendment rights argue that such a possibility is overblown and not likely to occur. But tell that to the parents of a thirteen-year-old Kentucky girl who was found in Los Angeles after being lured there by a grown-up cyberpal. Already, approximately a dozen high-profile cases have been documented in which children have been seduced or lured into situations where they were victimized.

One mother was shocked to find that her twelve-year-old daughter had been surfing the dark side of the Net. "It seems my sweet and innocent baby, my A-student, piano-playing teacher's favorite and her buddies had been sending messages such as 'Anyone out there want to talk to a hot babe?' and 'Sizzling F wants to talk to sexy M.'"[3] When she and her husband downloaded some of their daughter's e-mail, they found descriptions and pictures that most parents would find both shocking and offensive.

How Pervasive Is Cyberporn?

A recent study by Carnegie Mellon, *Marketing Pornography on the Information Superhighway*, provides the best documented evidence so far of the growing interest in cyberporn. Although the study has its critics and is not without its flaws, it nevertheless lays to rest the argument that cyberporn is a minor problem. The researchers pulled together elaborate computer records of online activity and reached the following conclusions:[4]

- There's a lot of pornography online. During their 18-month study, Carnegie Mellon researchers found 917,410 sexually explicit pictures, descriptions, stories, and clips. On the Usenet newsgroups where these digitized images are stored, they found that 83.5 percent of the pictures were pornographic.
- Online pornography is popular. Sexually explicit forums are the most popular areas on computer online services. At one university, thirteen of the forty most frequently visited newsgroups had names such as alt.sex.stories, rec.arts.erotica, and alt.sex.bondage.
- Online porn is big business. Nearly three-fourths (71 percent) of the sexually explicit images surveyed originate from adult bulletin-board systems (BBS), which attempt to lure customers to additional collections of cyberporn. The purveyors charge monthly fees and take credit card numbers for individual images. The five largest adult BBS systems have annual revenues in excess of $1 million.
- Online porn is everywhere. Carnegie Mellon researchers obtained records of Internet users and BBS operators. They found individual consumers in at least two thousand cities, in all fifty states, and in forty countries around the world.
- Most consumers of cyberporn are male. Women do

participate in "chat" rooms and other bulletin boards, but researchers have found, in fact, that 98.9 percent of the consumers of cyberporn images are men.

- Cyberporn is more than naked women. Demand for images goes far beyond what can be found in a bookstore magazine rack. Pedophilia, bestiality, bondage, and sadomasochism make up a majority of the images. Many of the images are too offensive to even describe here.

Congressional Action

The impact of some of these images on public policy has been significant. In the summer of 1995, Senators James Exon (D-Neb.) and Dan Coats (R-Ind.) proposed a revision to the Communications Decency Act. The bill would have extended existing dial-a-porn regulations to computer networks, outlaw obscene material, and impose fines of up to $100,000 and prison terms of up to two years on anyone who knowingly makes "indecent" material available to children under eighteen.

The bill languished—until Senator Exon produced his "blue book." Inside were some shocking images he'd had a friend download from some of the forums. "I knew it was bad," Senator Exon said. "But then when I got on there, it made *Playboy* and *Hustler* look like Sunday-school stuff."[5] He printed the images and stuffed them in a blue folder. Exon asked colleagues to stop by his desk on the Senate floor to see them. When the floor debate was over, the bill passed 84 to 16. The bill did not fare well in the House of Representatives, however, because of concerns about First Amendment rights.

Senator Patrick Leahy (D-Vt.) and Representative Ron

Klink (D-Pa.) introduced legislation that would order the Justice Department to study the problem of pornography on the Internet and propose solutions to Congress. As of this writing, that legislation has done little to curb porn on the Internet.

The argument for governmental regulation of cyberporn is simple. Currently, the federal government regulates dial-a-porn calls that take place over interstate phone lines. If it is constitutional to federally regulate audio sex transmitted over interstate phone lines, isn't it also constitutional to federally regulate video sex transmitted over those same interstate phone lines that are connected to modems and computers? The constitutional argument is sound.

What Can Parents Do?

The Internet is a wonderful marketplace of ideas and information, so most parents don't want to pull the plug on computer services. But parents do want to protect their kids from the seamier side of the Net. Here are a few suggestions:[6]

1. Use an online service that offers features to block pornographic sites. Many commercial services (e.g., CompuServe, America Online, Prodigy) have mechanisms to restrict access to areas that are inappropriate for children. Inquire about these mechanisms when you register with a service.

2. Block cyberporn with software. Also available is special software that can screen and block areas that children might try to investigate. SurfWatch is a software program that automatically blocks access to the approximately one thousand sexual hot spots on the Internet. Net Nanny is another program that

allows a parent or guardian to monitor everything that passes through the computer. If it detects an offending phrase in an online chat room, the program automatically disconnects the computer.[7]

3. Create a children's checklist. Ensure that your child knows the do's and don'ts of online computing. Never give out personal information (address, phone number). Never arrange a face-to-face meeting. Always remember that the person online might not be what he or she claims to be.

4. Watch your kids. Hover around your kids when they are online. Ask them to teach you some things about Internet features and maneuvering. Keep the family computer in a central location so that you have a better opportunity to see what your kids are doing and communicating. Notice when they are on the computer. Excessive use late at night might be an indication of a problem.

Many members of Congress have tried to pass legislation to curb pornography on the Internet. A nearly invisible, electronic river of pornographic slime flows toward our homes and communities with little regulation. Parents can do only so much, and Congress cannot shirk its responsibility to regulate this menace.

Until then, however, parents must do what they can to prevent these explicit images from invading their homes and perverting their children. We must stand for purity and righteousness and protect our children by fighting the insidious influence of cyberporn in our society.

5

Privacy Issues

Kerby Anderson

We tend to take privacy for granted—until we lose it. Then we think about how someone invaded our privacy, often incrementally. This chapter concentrates on the ways we have lost our privacy. Most, but not all, of the intrusions into our lives come from government. Businesses also buy and sell information about us every day. Most of us would be shocked to find out how much personal information about us is in databases around the country.

Consider a recent session of Congress. During that session of Congress no extended debate on issues related to privacy ever occurred. Granted, not a lot of debate occurred on a number of issues, but the lack of debate on this fundamental concern shows how far down the road we have gone in relinquishing privacy. No debate occurred, for example, on proposals such as the national ID card, the medical ID number, the Clinton administration encryption policy, and the expansion of the FBI's wiretap capability.

Some of those proposals were defeated—at least for now. The national ID card was defeated, for example, not because Congress debated the matter but because thousands of Americans wrote letters and made phone calls. Meanwhile, plans by the Clinton administration to develop a medical ID number were put on hold, but the plan could resurface at any time.

Most other such steps that lead to reduced privacy, however, are moving ahead. Congress gave the FBI permission to use "roving wiretap surveillance," meaning that the next time you use a pay phone at your local grocery store, it might be tapped merely because there's a criminal suspect within the area. In California, a wiretap order authorized surveillance on 350 phones for more than two years. In another case, five pay phones were tapped, and 131,000 conversations were intercepted.

Recently, the Federal Communications Commission mandated that cell phone and other wireless telephone companies track the location of their customers from the time a call is initiated until the time it is terminated. By locating the cell site the person is using, government can pinpoint the location of every citizen who uses a cell phone.

A discussion of these and other examples relative to privacy follows. First, however, why is privacy even a topic of discussion? Whenever someone cries for privacy, another person is sure to ask, "What do you have to hide?" The question confuses privacy and secrecy. I may not have anything I want to keep secret, but I'm not excited about the government listening to every one of my phone conversations. You might not want your future boss to know that you have a genetic predisposition to breast cancer. You might not want a telemarketing company to know what you purchased recently. As soon as the company has this information, it can hire someone to call you at home to try to sell you more.

The point is, each day we lose a bit of our privacy. And we'll continue to do so unless we insist on limits to the invasion of our privacy.

National ID Card

One method by which communist leaders controlled their citizenry was through issuing internal passports. Citizens had to carry these passports at all times and present them to authorities upon demand. The passports were required for travel within the country, to live in another part of the country, or to apply for a job.

In 1998, the Department of Transportation (DOT) called for the establishment of a national ID system by October 2000. The idea was presented as a move merely toward standardizing throughout the nation the information contained on ID cards and drivers' licenses. Many people viewed it, however, as a move toward a national passport to allow the government to "check up" on its citizens.

The history of the DOT's national ID system can be traced back to 1996. That year, Congress passed the Illegal Immigration Reform and Immigrant Responsibility Act, which charged the federal Department of Transportation with establishing national requirements for birth certificates and drivers' licenses. That same year the Kennedy-Kassebaum health-care law implied that in the future Americans, in order to receive Medicare or Medicaid, may be required to produce a state-issued ID that conforms to federal specifications.

If you think that standardized ID cards are reminiscent of Big Brother or even the mark of the Beast, then you have company. Congressman Ron Paul believes that the Department of Transportation regulations would adversely affect Americans. He says, "Under the current state of the law, the citizens of states which have drivers' licenses that do not conform to the federal standards by October 1, 2000, will find themselves essentially stripped of their ability to participate in life as we know it."[1]

Congressman Paul added, "On that date, Americans will not be able to get a job, open a bank account, apply for Social Security or Medicare, exercise their Second Amendment rights, or even take an airplane flight, unless they can produce a state-issued ID that conforms to the federal specifications."[2]

The law orders, among other things, that the Attorney General conduct pilot programs in which the state driver's license includes a "machine-readable" Social Security number; that a Social Security card be developed that uses magnetic strips, holograms, and integrated circuits; that states collect Social Security numbers from all applicants for various licenses; that states transmit the name, address, and Social Security number of every new worker to a Directory of New Hires.

The good news is that the work by Congressmen Ron Paul and Bob Barr paid off, and the attempt to create a national ID card was stopped—for now. But it is likely to surface again. The push to establish a federal database for Americans has existed for some time. And each person's federally mandated ID card would carry information that could be linked to a federal database. And although such a link would help the government catch illegal aliens, it could also be used to track law-abiding American citizens.

Tracking down illegal aliens and standardizing licenses are worthy goals. But the ends do not justify the means. Sometimes in the midst of political debate, citizens must ask themselves how much they value their freedom and privacy.

Congressman Barr says, "Novelists Aldous Huxley and George Orwell have given us countless reasons why we shouldn't trade our privacy for any benefit, no matter how worthwhile it sounds."[3] In the end, we must ask, "At what cost? Is it worth trading our privacy for the benefits that government promises?"

Medical ID Number

While the Department of Transportation is moving ahead with plans for a national ID card, the Department of Health and Human Services is working to assign everyone a lifetime medical ID number. The purpose of the ID number is to facilitate accurate record keeping as patients change doctors and health plans. The identification was required in a 1996 law that guarantees workers continued access to health coverage even if they change jobs.

It has been proposed to simply use Social Security numbers as medical ID numbers. But doing that could give credit card companies and other organizations access to medical records, which raises a concern over the privacy of such records. And maintaining privacy is exactly the point. Even a secure number still poses the potential to give everyone—from insurance companies to computer hackers—access to medical histories.

One doctor expressed his concern that tracing a "unique patient identifier could lead to a central data base." He fears that "someone without permission could break into those records."[4] But even if records are secure, doctors fear that patients will withhold embarrassing information for fear that someone else might access their records.

Robert Gellman, an information policy consultant, said at a recent hearing, "Once everyone's required to use a government-issued health identification card, it may become impossible for any American citizen to walk down the street without being forced to produce that card on demand by a policeman."[5]

Why are so many people concerned? Perhaps past history is an indication. One of the features of Hillary Clinton's national health-care plan was a federal database of every American's medical records. During his state of the union address, President Clinton waved a card with a "unique identifier number" that would give government bureaucrats and health-care providers easy computer access to everyone's medical history.

Although the American people rejected that plan back in 1993 and 1994, the government is still moving ahead with a plan to give every American a "unique identifier number" and to compile medical records into a federal database. Several years ago, the proponents of a medical card and number linked to a federal database argued that it would aid in health-care planning and eliminating fraud by health-care providers. The American people feared, however, that it would end medical privacy and increase federal control over health care.

That fear is justified. Consider what already occurs in a system *without* a medical ID number. For example, a banker on a county health-care board called due the mortgages of people suffering with cancer. Before Primary Day, a congresswoman's medical records were leaked, revealing a bout of depression. And a number of drugstore chains sell to marketing firms the names, addresses, and ailments of their customers.

The Hippocratic Oath says, "That whatsoever I shall see or hear of the lives of men, which is not fitting to be spoken . . . I shall keep inviolably secret." Current attempts by the federal bureaucracy to standardize and centralize medical information are presented as a way to make health-care delivery more effective and efficient. But those measures also have the potential to invade our privacy and threaten doctor-patient confidentiality. Perhaps this proposal needs a second opinion.

Encryption

Encryption is an unfamiliar word. It's a big word that has created a big issue.

Encryption is a relatively new technology that enables you to have private phone conversations and send e-mail messages that are secure. Encryption codes your words so that they cannot be deciphered by people listening in on your conversation or reading your e-mail.

Nosy people already can listen in on your wireless phone calls (cellular or cordless phones). And they can intercept and read your e-mail. Sending e-mail without encryption is like mailing a postcard—everyone can read it along the way. And we all know that people will do exactly that. If you've ever had a phone on a party line, you know that people listen in.

What you may not know is that various members of the Clinton administration (such as Attorney General Janet Reno and FBI Director Louis Freeh) were demanding the authority to read encrypted messages. Remember, however, that the Fourth Amendment guarantees citizens freedom from unreasonable searches and seizures. Nevertheless, these and other law enforcement officers believed that they have the right to open your mail.

They were asking, in essence, for the key to the code. When you send a message in code, you need a key to enable you to encode the message and the recipient needs the same key to decode the message. The Clinton administration was demanding access to all encryption keys. This would be like giving the government the power to steam open all of the letters we send in the mail. It is more usual to see this level of surveillance in totalitarian countries. If government has the key, then it could call up information on you, your family, your medical records, your bank records, your credit card purchases, and your e-mail messages to all of your friends and relatives.

Even more disturbing was the recent attempt by government to limit access by American citizens to powerful encryption software. A study from the Cato Institute states, "People living outside the United States find it amusing and perplexing that U.S. law regulates the distribution of strong encryption."[6] Critics of the administration's policy pointed out that true criminals (terrorists, drug dealers, the mafia) are unlikely to use anything less than the strongest encryption for their communication and data storage. It is unlikely, too, that government will have a key to that level of encryption. Meanwhile, the average citizen must use weak encryption to protect private data and run the risk that the government will someday have a key to access it.

In the computer age, everyone wants encryption. Citizens want private communication; businesses want to prevent billing records and personnel records from falling into the wrong hands; consumers don't want their credit card numbers widely distributed. We need strong encryption software, and government should not be given a key to the messages we send.

Privacy and Your Life

Dave Ballert thought that he was being a savvy consumer when he attempted to download a copy of his credit report from a Web site. He hadn't checked it in a while and thought that it was worth paying the eight bucks. But when the report arrived a few minutes later, it wasn't his. It was a report for someone in California. The next thing he knew, he received a call from someone at the *Washington Post* who said that they had received his report.[7] The Web site halted access later, but the damage was already done. How would you like for a major newspaper to have a copy of your credit report?

Or consider the case of the Social Security Administration, which provided earnings information to individuals via the Internet. The information for individual card holders, however, was being accessed by other persons as well. After more than a month of allowing unfettered access by disgruntled employees, ex-spouses, and their attorneys, the Social Security Administration finally pulled the plug.

Such is life in the cyberage. More and more people are seeing their privacy violated and feel financially and personally violated. What used to be considered private records are now being made public at an alarming rate.

What should we do? First, don't give out personal information. Assume that any information you divulge will end up on a database somewhere. Phone solicitors, application forms, and warranty cards all ask for information you might not want to give out. Be circumspect about what you disclose.

Second, live your life above reproach. Philippians 2:14–15 says, "Do all things without grumbling or disputing, that you may prove yourselves to be blameless and innocent, children of God above reproach in the midst of a crooked and perverse generation, among whom you appear as lights in the world." First Timothy 3:2 says that an elder must be "above reproach," an attribute that should describe all of us. If you live a life of integrity, you don't have to fear what might be made public.

Third, exercise discretion, especially when you use

e-mail. Too many people assume that they have a one-on-one relationship with someone through the Internet, but the message that you send might be forwarded to other people. One Web site provider says, "A good rule of thumb: don't send any e-mail that you wouldn't want your mother to read."[8]

Finally, get involved. When you think that your privacy has been violated, take the time to complain. Let the offending person or organization know your concerns. The offender may fail to apply the same rules of privacy and confidentiality on a computer that apply in real life. Your complaint might change a behavior and have a positive effect.

Track congressional legislation and write letters to your elected officials. Many governmental policies pose a threat to our privacy, and further threats will no doubt be initiated in Congress. Citizens should understand that bureaucrats and legislators are in the business of collecting information and will continue to do so unless we set appropriate limits.

Most Americans are unaware of the growing threats to their privacy posed by government and private industry. Most Americans would not like to turn over private information. Most Americans don't realize that they already have.

Eternal vigilance is the price of freedom. We must continue to monitor the threats to our privacy from both the public and private sectors.

6

Online Affairs

Kerby Anderson

Experts say that the Internet is becoming a breeding ground for adultery. That assertion compels a discussion of online affairs.

Peggy Vaughn, author of *The Monogamy Myth*, works with America Online, and is an expert on problems caused by infidelity. She predicts that one "role of the Internet in the future will be as a source of affairs."[1] She's writing a second book on the subject of adultery and says that she could base half of it just on the letters she receives from people who started an affair online.

An online affair (or cyberaffair) is an intimate or sexually explicit Internet communication between a married person and someone other than his or her spouse. This communication usually takes place through an online service such as America Online or Compuserve. Participants who wind up in affairs start out by visiting a chat room to begin a group conversation and then typically move into a one-to-one mode of communication. Chat room categories range from "single and liking it" to "married and flirting" to "naked on the keyboard."

Women in chat rooms are often surprised at what develops in a fairly short period of time. At first, the conversation is stimulating although flirtatious. But women often find that the questions and comments quickly become increasingly sexual. Even if the comments don't turn personal, women find themselves sharing intimate information about themselves and their relationships that they would never share with someone in person. Vaughn says, "Stay-at-home moms in chat rooms are sharing all this personal stuff they are hiding from their partners." She finds that the intensity of women's online relationships can "quickly escalate into thinking they have found a soulmate."[2]

Online affairs differ from physical, real-world affairs in some ways but are similar in others. Cyberaffairs are based upon written communication in which people, hiding behind the cloak of anonymity, may feel more free to express themselves than they would in person. The communication frequently becomes sexually graphic and kinky, a circumstance that would not occur if the conversation were taking place in person. Participants in an online affair will often tell their life stories and their innermost secrets. They will also create a new persona, become sexually adventurous, and pretend to be different than they are.

Pretending is a major theme in cyberaffairs. Men claim to be professionals (doctors, lawyers) who work out every day in the gym. And they universally claim that if their wives met their needs, they wouldn't be sex shopping on the Internet.

Women claim to be slim, sexy, and adventurous. The anonymity of the Internet allows them to divulge (or even create) their wildest fantasies. In fact, their frank talk and flirtation pays great dividends in the number of men in a chat room who want to talk to them and get together with them.

Just as the Internet has become a new source of

pornography, it has also become a new source for initiating affairs. And in their wakes, relationships online frequently leave pain, heartbreak, and even divorce. Even though these online affairs don't involve sex, they can be nonetheless very intense and create a threat to marriage.

Current Statistics on Adultery

In an earlier book, *Marriage, Family, and Sexuality*,[3] I discussed some of the statistics concerning adultery. A multitude of studies have updated some of those numbers, all reaching similar conclusions.

Adultery is becoming more common, and researchers find that women are as likely as men to have an affair. A 1983 study found that 29 percent of married people under twenty-five had had an affair with no statistical difference between the number of men and women who early in life chose to be unfaithful to their spouses.[4] By comparison, only 9 percent of spouses under the age of twenty-five in the 1950s had been involved in extramarital sex. Another study concluded that by age forty about 50 to 65 percent of husbands and 45 to 55 percent of wives become involved in an extramarital affair.[5]

Affairs are usually more than a one-time event. A 1987 study surveyed two hundred men and women and found that their affairs lasted an average of two years.[6] In fact, affairs go through transitions over time. They may begin as romantic, sexual, or emotional relationships and develop into intimate friendships. Affairs that become friendships can last decades or a lifetime.

Online affairs differ from other affairs in that they might not involve a physical component, but the emotional attachment is still present. Cybersex develops because of the dual attraction of attention and anonymity. Someone who has been ignored by a spouse (or at least perceives that he or she is ignored) suddenly becomes the center of attention in a chat room or a one-on-one e-mail exchange. A woman finds it exciting, even intoxicating, that all of these men want to talk to her. And they are eager to hear what she says and needs.

Anonymity feeds this intoxication because the person on the other end of the cyberaffair is unknown. He or she can be as beautiful and intelligent as your dreams can imagine. The fantasy is fueled by the lack of information and the anonymity. No one in cyberland has bad breath, a bald head, love handles, or a bad temper. The sex is the best that you can imagine. Men are warm, sensitive, caring, and communicative. Women are daring, sensual, and erotic.

Is it all too good to be true? Of course it is. Cyberaffairs are only make-believe. When cyberlovers meet, they usually experience a major letdown. No real person can compete with a dream lover. No marriage can compete with a cyberaffair. But then an online affair can't really compete with a real relationship that provides true friendship and marital intimacy.

Nevertheless, online affairs are seductive. An Internet addict calls out to a spouse "one more minute" just as an alcoholic justifies "one more drink." Cyberaffairs provide an opportunity to become another person, and chat with distant and invisible neighbors in the high-tech limbo of cyberspace. Social and emotional needs are met, flirting is allowed and even encouraged, and an illusion of intimacy feeds the addiction that has caught so many unsuspecting Internet surfers.

Motivations for Affairs

Affairs, whether real life or online—usually develop because the illicit relationship meets various social and psychological needs. Self-esteem needs are often at the top of the list and are met through the needy person's being known, understood, and accepted by his or her lover. Psychologists say that those needs are enhanced through talking intimately about feelings, thoughts, and the needs themselves. Such talk can take place both in person or through the Internet.

Although online affairs might not involve a physical component, the emotional attachment can be just as strong and even more overwhelming than real-life affairs. And when any affair ends, severing the attachment usually leaves participants in emotional pain.

Men and women have affairs for different reasons. Research has shown that women seek affairs to be loved, have a friend, and feel needed. Men seek affairs for sexual fulfillment, friendship, and fun.[7]

Women report feeling thrilled by their lovers' interest in them physically, emotionally, and intellectually. They are also excited about the chance to know a different man (how he thinks and feels) and to feel intimate with their lovers through talking openly about their feelings. When the affair ends, however, women feel a great deal of guilt with regard to their husbands and children. They also regret the deceit that accompanied the affair.

Men report feeling excited about the sexual experience of the affair. Men typically try to control their feelings in regard to the affair, often limiting emotional involvement with their lovers. And although men claim that they don't allow the affair to compete with their feelings for their wives, they nonetheless feel guilt and regret over deceit when an affair ends, but less so than do most women.

According to statistics, the percentage of women who have extramarital sex has increased over the last few decades. In 1953, Alfred Kinsey found that 29 percent of married women admitted to at least one affair.[8] A *Psychology Today* survey in 1970 reported that 36 percent of their female readers had had extramarital sex.[9] One study in 1987 found that 70 percent of women surveyed had been involved in an affair.[10]

Women who are employed full-time outside of the home are more likely to have an affair than are full-time homemakers. Several studies reach this same conclusion. One study found that 47 percent of wives who were employed full-time and 27 percent of full-time homemakers had been involved in an affair before they were forty years old.[11] And *New Woman* magazine found that 57 percent of employed wives who had an affair met their lover at work.[12]

Contrary to conventional wisdom, an affair will not help your marriage. In 1975, Linda Wolfe published *Playing Around* after having studied twenty-one women who were having affairs to keep their marriages intact.[13] Many of these women reasoned that if they could meet their own needs, their marriages would be more successful. Many of them said that they were desperately lonely. Others were afraid, believing that their husbands did not love them or were not committed to their marriage. Five years after the initial study, only three of the twenty-one women were still married.

Adultery can destroy a marriage, whether it involves a physical affair or an online affair.

Preventing an Affair

Over forty years, family therapist Frank Pittman counseled ten thousand couples, about seven thousand of whom had experienced infidelity. The suggestions below, to which I have added additional material, are based upon Pittman's book *Private Lies: Infidelity and the Betrayal of Intimacy*.[14] He lists nineteen specific suggestions, of which eight will be touched upon here.

First, accept the possibility of being sexually attracted to another person and of having sexual fantasies. Pittman believes that we should acknowledge that such thoughts can occur so that we aren't frightened by them and thus deny them. But he also says that we shouldn't act upon them.

Second, we should associate with monogamous people, who, says Pittman, "make a good support system." To state it negatively, "Do not be deceived: 'Bad company corrupts good morals'" (1 Cor. 15:33).

Third, work on your marriage. Pittman says to keep your marriage sexy, and work to be intimate with your spouse. He also says to make marriage an important part of your identity. "Carry your marriage with you wherever you go."

Fourth, be realistic about your marriage. Pittman says, "Don't expect your marriage to make you happy. See your partner as a source of comfort rather than a cause of unhappiness." Accept the reality of marriage; it isn't always beautiful. Also accept that both you and your spouse are imperfect.

Fifth, keep the marriage equal. Share parenting duties. "If not, one partner will become the full-time parent, and the other will become a full-time child" without responsibilities, who seeks to be taken care of. And keep the relationship equal. Pittman says, "The more equal it is, the more both partners will respect and value it."

Sixth, if you aren't already married, be careful in your choice of a marriage partner. Marry someone who believes in and has a family history of monogamy. Pittman says,

"It is a bad idea to become the fifth husband of a woman who has been unfaithful to her previous four." Also, marry someone who respects and likes the opposite sex. Otherwise, "They will get over the specialness of you yourself and eventually consider you as part of a gender they dislike."

Seventh, call home every day when you travel. "Otherwise, you begin to have a separate life." And stay faithful. "If you want your partner to [stay faithful], it is a good idea to stay faithful yourself." And ensure that you are open, honest, and authentic. Lies and deception create a secret life that can allow an affair to occur.

Finally, don't overreact or exaggerate the consequences of an affair if one occurs. Pittman says, "It doesn't mean there will be a divorce, murder, or suicide. Catch yourself and work your way back into the marriage."

Affairs can destroy a marriage. Take the time to affair-proof your marriage so that you avoid the pain, guilt, and regret that inevitably result. And if you have fallen into an affair, work your way back and rebuild your marriage.

Consequences of Affairs

When God commanded, "You shall not commit adultery" (Exod. 20:14), He did so for our own good. Significant social, psychological, and spiritual consequences attend adultery.

A major social cost is divorce. An affair that is discovered does not have to lead to divorce, but often it does. Only about one-third of couples remain together after the discovery of adultery.

And it's not surprising that the divorce rate is higher among people who have affairs. Annette Lawson, author of *Adultery: An Analysis of Love and Betrayal*, found that spouses who did not have affairs had the lowest rate of divorce. Women who had multiple affairs (especially if they started early in the marriage) had the highest rate of divorce.

A lesser known fact is that those who divorce because of an affair rarely marry the person with whom they are having the affair. For example, Jan Halper's study of successful men (executives, entrepreneurs, professionals) found that very few men who have affairs divorce their wives and marry their lovers. Only 3 percent of the forty-one hundred successful men surveyed eventually married their lovers.[15] Pittman found that the divorce rate among those who do marry their lovers was 75 percent. The reasons for such a high rate include the injection of reality, feelings of guilt, unrealistic expectations, and an increase in distrust. Affairs destroy trust—trust in marriage and trust in the new spouse. It's not surprising that new marriages formed after an affair have such a high divorce rate. If your new spouse cheated before, what guarantee do you have that this person won't begin to cheat on you?

The psychological consequences of an affair are also significant, even if they are sometimes more difficult to discern. People who pursue an affair often do so to meet needs for self-esteem, but affairs often further erode those feelings by violating trust, intimacy, and stability in a marriage relationship. Affairs do not stabilize a marriage, they upset it.

Finally, affairs have spiritual consequences. We not only grieve the Lord by our actions, we disgrace the Lord as we become one more statistic of moral failure within the body of Christ. Affairs threaten the sacred marriage bond between spouses, bringing guilt into our lives and shame into our marriage and family. Affairs extract a tremendous price in both our lives and in the lives of those we love and hold dear.

Consider, too, some of the long-term consequences. Affairs can lead to unwanted pregnancies. According to one report, "Studies of blood typing show that as many as 1 out of every 10 babies born in North America is not the offspring of the mother's husband."[16] Affairs can also result in sexually transmitted diseases such as syphilis, chlamydia, herpes, or even AIDS. Many of these diseases are incurable, will last for a lifetime, and may even be deadly.

Adultery is dangerous, and so are online affairs. The popularity of the recent movie *You've Got Mail* has helped feed the fantasy that you are writing to Tom Hanks or Meg Ryan. In almost every case, however, nothing could be further from the truth. An online affair might more appropriately be titled *Fatal Attraction*.

7

Human Cloning

Ray Bohlin

O ne sheep caused quite a stir. In February 1997, it was announced that Dolly the sheep was the first mammal cloned from adult cells. A storm of publicity and controversy erupted. Many people wondered about the purpose of animal cloning and the possibilities that such a success held for further animal applications. Other people were more concerned about the application of cloning to human beings.

Is Dolly Really a Clone?

If we can clone sheep, can we clone humans? If so, should we clone humans? Why should we clone humans? Should humans be cloned to provide a baby for childless, infertile couples? Should we clone humans for embryo research? Should we clone humans to make extra copies of people with good genes? Would clones have a soul?

Although I answered these and other questions about human cloning in my article "Can Humans Be Cloned Like Sheep?"[1] (available from Probe Ministries or on our Web site), in retrospect, I realize that one question was virtually ignored at the outset: Is Dolly a true clone?

This question is legitimate and should have been more obvious. After all, Dolly was the only success amid 276 failures. Of the 277 cell fusions made, only 29 were growing as embryos. All 29 embryos were implanted into 13 ewes with a result of only one pregnancy and one live birth. Dolly really beat the odds. Also, Dolly was not cloned from a currently living adult. Dolly's older twin had been dead for several years. Some of her tissues were harvested and kept frozen in the lab, so no live animal was available with which to compare Dolly.

Dolly's authenticity was formally challenged in a January 30, 1998, letter to the editor of the journal *Science*.[2] The authors offered seven reasons for skepticism concerning Dolly's identity as a clone of an adult cell. First, Dolly was the sole result of cloning experimentation; no other adult clone has issued from the Roslin Institute or any other laboratory. Scientific experiments, in order to achieve peer acceptance, should be repeatable. Also, although the fact was omitted from the original paper, researchers had learned that the original sheep had been pregnant when the tissues were removed, raising the possibility that Dolly was cloned from a fetal cell rather than from an adult cell. In addition, the questioning scientists called for additional genetic tests to establish Dolly's identity.

Although Ian Wilmut, the Scottish scientist who is Dolly's cocreator, admitted that Dolly might be a one-in-a-million fluke, he and others were busy performing genetic tests to establish fully that Dolly was an authentic clone from an adult cell. Other labs had so far failed, after hundreds of tries, to duplicate Wilmut's success. This failure might not be unusual because Dolly was the only success of nearly three hundred nuclear transfers, and the real odds might be as high as one in one thousand. Wilmut might indeed have gotten lucky to achieve success after only three hundred tries.[3]

A pair of papers in the British journal *Nature* remedied much of the concern over Dolly's authenticity.[4] Microsatellite DNA and DNA fingerprinting analyses demonstrated conclusively that Dolly was an identical DNA copy of the cells of a six-year-old ewe and not a clone of the fetus carried inside that ewe.

Cloning Mice Makes Cloning Humans More Feasible

Even with the success of cloning sheep, many people doubted that the technology used to produce Dolly could be applied to humans. This skepticism was largely the result of the universal failure to clone mice from adult cells.

Mice have a number of advantages as experimental animals for cloning. The gestation time in mice is very short (a matter of weeks), their embryos are easier to manipulate than those of sheep and cows, and their genetics are already well understood.[5] But also widely recognized, the early development of mice and sheep is significantly different. In sheep, the DNA in the newly formed nucleus remains dormant for several days, which, researchers suspected, provides time for the DNA to be reprogrammed from its original function to embryonic functions. Mice, on the other hand, begin using the DNA in the newly formed nucleus after just twenty-four hours. Researchers thought that this time might prove to be insufficient for the DNA to be reprogrammed.

This problem, too, has been overcome and in dramatic fashion. In July 1998, *Nature* published results by T. Wakayama, working in Hawaii, that documented the cloning of mice.[6] And not just one mouse but more than fifty mice. Three successive generations were cloned, raising the conundrum that the "grandmother" was the twin sister of the "granddaughters."[7]

But what did Wakayama and his colleagues do that was different to bring about success? Strangely enough, no one is really sure. Apart from a few tricks of timing, the major difference seems to be a cell type that no one had used before, and it worked! As an aside, Wakayama tried other adult mouse cells (neurons and testicular cells) that brought about only the usual negative results.

But the Hawaiian researchers also tried cumulus cells, a nongrowing group of cells that surround an egg cell after it is released from the ovaries. This effort confirmed the suspicion that adult cells must be quiescent or nongrowing to be successful in cloning experiments. Nonetheless, using cumulus cells, the nuclear transfer technique employed by Wakayama was successful between 2 and 3 percent of the time. This rate of success is ten times better than the technique that led to Dolly, but it is still very low, making the process tedious.

The success with cumulus cells is why the first cloned mouse was named Cumulina. Also interesting is that, to date, only cells from females have been successful in cloning attempts. If all that is needed is a quiescent adult cell, an egg, and a womb, male involvement isn't really necessary. Perhaps it's best not to speculate what this could mean in the future.

For many people, the real significance of successful mouse cloning techniques is its application to humans. The early stages of embryonic development are very similar in mice and humans. Therefore, many people believed that because cloning mice seemed next to impossible because of the early onset of DNA activity in mice and humans, cloning humans would also remain technologically impossible. Cumulina and her sisters have changed all that.

For What Will Animal Cloning Be Used?

So now we can clone sheep and mice. Since 1998, pigs, cattle, goats, and cats have been added to the list. Apart from the possibilities for human benefit, what's the big deal? Why are scientists and pharmaceutical companies spending so much time and money trying to clone animals? Quite simply, the combination of the possible relief of human suffering from genetic disease and the potential to turn a handsome profit makes animal cloning nearly irresistible.

In the December 1998 issue of *Scientific American,* Ian Wilmut spells out some of the potential uses of animal cloning.[8] Cloning will be used principally to create large numbers of what are called transgenic animals, animals that are engineered genetically to contain genes from another species. Wilmut and his colleagues created Dolly in an attempt to discover a more reliable method of reproducing transgenic sheep.

Creating transgenic animals is very tedious, difficult, and risky work. The Roslin Institute and PPL Therapeutics, for whom Wilmut works, transferred into sheep the gene for human factor IX, a blood-clotting protein used to treat hemophilia. With the proper genetic enhancement, sheep will produce this blood-clotting factor in their milk, which can then be harvested and sold on the market for hemophiliacs. The first transgenic sheep produced this way, Polly, was born in the summer of 1997. It is actually simpler to clone Polly than to create another transgenic sheep through gene transfer.

Cloning offers many other possibilities for reproducing other kinds of transgenic animals. One is the production of animals containing transgenic organs suitable for organ transplants into humans. Pig organs are just about the right size for transplantation into humans. The human immune system would, however, quickly and severely reject a pig heart, or liver, or kidney. But if the right human genes could be transferred into pigs, the organs they produce would be recognized by a human body as a human organ and not as a pig organ. The same problems of immune rejection associated with any organ transplant between humans would still exist, but those are much more manageable once the problem of cross-species immune rejection is solved. Thousands of people die every year waiting for organs to become available. Cloning such transgenic animals could create a large and renewable source of organs for transplant.

Transgenic animals could also be created for research in human genetic diseases. Transferring defective human genes into appropriate animal hosts could produce more workable research vehicles for discovering new treatments and cures not possible using human subjects. Cloning of transgenic animals may also prove useful to create cells that are helpful in treating human diseases such as Parkinson's disease, diabetes, and muscular dystrophy. In addition, cloning could be used to produce highly productive herds of sheep, cows, and pigs from animals that are already known to be excellent milk, meat, and leather producers.

Obviously, the uses of animal cloning seem limited only by imagination. If one is already opposed to the use of animals in experiments or even their use for food, these ideas are, of course, fraught with ethical difficulties. The

Lord Himself, however, produced the first skins for humans in Genesis 3:21 and later, after the Flood, the Lord allowed animals to be used for food (Gen. 9:2–4). Although we must take the utmost care to ensure that God's creatures, for whom we have been given responsibility (Gen. 1:26–28) do not suffer needlessly, the Lord clearly allows us to use animals to enhance our own lives, even if it costs them theirs.

New Uses for Human Embryo Research?

What if I told you that recent breakthroughs in human genetic research might make it possible to offer dramatic treatment to patients with Alzheimer's, Parkinson's, heart disease, diabetes, spinal cord injury, and a host of other degenerative diseases? In some cases, these treatments might actually effect a cure and would not require the use of cells obtained from aborted fetuses. Have I got your attention?

The November 6, 1998, issue of *Science* announced the first successful attempts to cultivate human embryonic stem cells that have the potential to treat all the preceding diseases and more.[9] The success comes, however, with its own set of difficult and perhaps more serious ethical concerns.

First, just what are embryonic stem cells? Stems from plant seedlings give rise to all sorts of different structures such as trunks, branches, leaves, flowers, and eventually seeds and fruits. Animal embryonic stem cells do much the same thing. Stem cells have the potential to grow into just about any tissue that is present in the adult organism. Researchers call this potential *totipotency,* meaning that they are potent to produce all tissues. Embryonic stem cells have been isolated from mice since the early 1980s.

Such research has been impossible in humans for ethical reasons; stem cells come only from embryos in the earliest stages of development.

No one was willing simply to use embryos to obtain stem cells, thus killing the embryo, every time stem cells were needed. But stem cells can be isolated and cultivated in the laboratory, where they grow and divide and maintain their stem cell functions. These stem cell lines provide a continual supply of stem cells that can be used indefinitely without risk to further embryos. Stem cell line research was greeted with such comments as "extremely important," "very encouraging," and "a major technical achievement with great importance for human biology."[10]

What you might have noted in the preceding description is that a human embryo must still be used to create this stem cell line. In fact, the study reported in *Science* indicates that thirty-six embryos obtained from in vitro fertilization clinics in Madison, Wisconsin, and Israel were used to create five stem cell lines. The embryos were obtained with the consent of the individuals whose eggs and sperm were used to create them and the approval of the local institutional review board.

The major concern regards the legality of other labs' using these cells. Because of a ban on the use of federal funds for research involving tissues derived from human embryos, this research was carried out using private funds from Geron Corporation, a Menlo Park, California, biotechnology firm. The question is whether other labs currently funded by government grants can use these cells. As could be predicted, one researcher, in order to test and effect repeal of this restriction, quickly applied for grant money to use these stem cells.[11]

Proponents of stem cell research criticize the federal ban because it does not allow for government regulation and no guidelines have been issued for private research. I agree that the lack of guidelines for private industry is an oversight, but opening up government funding is not the answer. The ban should remain in force. Guidelines should be issued that forbid creating stem cell lines as long as human embryos are sacrificed to produce them.

Recent advances have shown that many of the benefits of stem cells can be achieved by using stem cells obtained from adult tissue.[12] Cells from adult tissue offer several advantages over embryonic stem cells. First, if the stem cells are to be used to treat a particular individual, the cells can be obtained from the very individual to be treated, thus avoiding rejection problems. Second, adult stem cells are more limited in their potentialities and therefore more controllable. And third, no embryos need be sacrificed to obtain these cells. I am not aware of anyone who is opposed to researching the full potential of adult stem cells. Research using animals as well as stem cells from adults should be encouraged to determine if stem cells could be produced by other means. Although research into curing a variety of genetic diseases is important, the end does not justify the means.

When President George W. Bush decided to open up federal funding for research on already existing human embryonic stem cell lines in August 2001, just about everyone was unhappy. Researchers and patient advocates complained that this will limit the available research if existing cell lines don't work out. The supply might not meet research demand. Pro-life groups, including this writer, were displeased because the decision implicitly approves the destruction of embryos used to create these

ES cell lines. They will cost researchers at least $5,000 per cell line. Therefore, to purchase them for research indirectly supports their creation.

Since both sides are unhappy, it was probably a good political decision, even if it was not the best ethics decision.

The Prospects for Human Cloning: The Enigma of Dr. Richard Seed

I am frequently asked, "How soon do you think the first human clone will be produced?" I usually respond that somewhere in the world within the next five to ten years, someone will announce the creation of the first human clone. But if we are to believe Dr. Richard Seed, the first human clone should have been produced by now. In December 1997, Seed, a physicist turned fertility specialist, announced that he intends to clone human beings. He said, "I know of at least fifteen people who want to clone humans, but haven't got quite up the nerve to do it."[13] When asked if he had the nerve, Seed replied, "I have the nerve."

Seed appeared in the news again in September 1998 when he announced his plans to clone himself in two years and that his wife agreed to carry the baby.[14] Seed reported that he had received hundreds of calls from individuals who want either themselves or their dying children cloned. Seed thinks that this is a first step to human immortality. On January 7, 1998, Seed affirmed on *ABC News Nightline* his remarks from a National Public Radio interview that cloning technology will allow us to "become one with God. We are going to have almost as much knowledge and almost as much power as God."[15]

You probably think that this guy is a kook. Why worry about him? Well, that's precisely why we need to pay attention to him. He has the ability; he perfected embryo transfers in humans. He certainly has the motivation and nerve, and he is still seeking the cash to finance his procedure. But if he is accurate in the number of calls he has received, money might not be a problem for long. And even if the U.S. Congress passes a bill banning human cloning, Seed has said that he will move his operation to Tijuana, Mexico.

People like Richard Seed are why I believe that someone somewhere in the world will produce a human clone very soon. But are we just going to throw up our hands and surrender, or will we continue to stand up for the sanctity of human life and the sacredness of the human embryo?

While Dr. Seed has not announced success on his promise to clone himself, he has new competition. In early 2001, two scientists announced their intent to open a human cloning clinic somewhere in the Mediterranean. Drs. Zavos and Antinori announced that they intended to achieve a human clone within two years. They said that they had clients (more than six hundred of them) lining up for the service and an unlimited supply of start-up cash.[16] Most people who have publicly indicated their interest in being cloned talked mostly about themselves and not the impact on the potential clone. For instance,

> Jack Barker, Minneapolis marketing specialist, 36, says, "I've come to the conclusion that I don't need a partner but can still have a child," he says. "A clone would be the perfect child to have because I know exactly what I'm getting."
>
> Cloning, he hopes, might even let him improve on the original: "I have had bad allergies and

asthma. It would be nice to have a kid like you but
with those improvements."[17]

Animal cloning raised numerous problems that pro-
voked recrimination from scientists who oppose any attempt to clone humans. If the clone survives to birth, most
of them are oversized, causing problems in the birthing
process. Some clones just suddenly die shortly after birth
because of numerous causes that appear to be related to
the cloning process.[18] These complications reveal risks for
the surrogate mother as well as the clone itself. The success rate for achieving a clone is about 2 to 3 percent,
indicating that for every successful clone, thirty to fifty
embryos would have to be implanted. This process would
require dozens of surrogate mothers.

The primary motivation for Antinori and his group is
the treatment of severe infertility. But even for this otherwise admirable goal, the risks and consequences must be
analyzed by not only scientists but also by society as a
whole. The bizarre cult group Raelians offers their cloning services (for $50,000) to bring back a deceased loved
one, principally a child. This inhumane attempt at grief
management even caught the ire of liberal columnist Ellen
Goodman, who concluded,

> Today, safety concerns alone are enough reason to
> support the Food and Drug Administration's role
> in policing the irresponsible human experiments
> done in the name of progress. But there is some-
> thing equally unethical about those hucksters of
> hope who sell cloning as an antidote to mourning.
> It is nothing but a dosage of denial.[19]

Bioethicist Arthur Caplan states,

> The short answer to the cloning question is that anybody who clones somebody today should be arrested. It would be barbaric human experimentation. It would be killing fetuses and embryos for no purpose, none, except for curiosity. But if you can't agree that that's wrong to do, and if the media can't agree to condemn rather than gawk, that's a condemnation of us all.[20]

If we don't think carefully and organize a cogent response to this threat to human dignity, the attitude of people like Professor James Robl at the University of Massachusetts at Amherst from an interview in a documentary on cloning will prevail:

> So, there is no clear-cut definition for what is life. And this is something, I think, that society is going to have to think about, is going to have to make some definitions, and those definitions may not be permanent, they may change as new technologies are developed. There is a fine line, and the line, at the early stages, is really based on your intention of what they are to be used for as opposed to necessarily what they are. So the question of what is life seems to change, I think, in people's minds based on what their own concerns are or their own interests are in how we might use whatever it is we are producing.[21]

Professor Robl calls for an entirely utilitarian ethic. Define life, he says, based solely on what new technologies are developed. If a new technology, such as cloning or human stem cell production from human embryos, becomes available but threatens human dignity, we simply redefine human life to encompass the new technology. This is the frightening specter of a brave new world. We must oppose it, and we must articulate why we do so.

8

Human Genome Project

Ray Bohlin

The project is complete! In February 2001, every medium—TV news, newspapers, radio, Internet news services, news magazines—expressed excitement about the completion of the Human Genome Project (HGP). This chapter explores this monumental achievement and what it means for the future of medicine and our understanding of ourselves.

What's All the Fuss About?

To appreciate the significance of the HGP, a brief overview of basic genetics is in order. The National Institutes of Health assumes that most adults are far more familiar with genetics than is the case. The educational video from HGP includes a three-minute review of such basic genetic processes as DNA packaging, transcription of DNA into message RNA, and the translation of message RNA into protein. When I played this short piece during a lecture for high school students and their parents, moms and dads were left in the dust.

It was, frankly, my intention that the parents be made aware of their own need for education. We can no longer afford to remain ignorant of genetic technologies. The HGP is only the beginning stages of a genetic revolution that will transform the way we diagnose and treat disease and how we may even alter our genetic structure. These new technologies bring with them numerous ethical and moral dilemmas that we have only begun to address and for which simple answers might not exist. If we don't take the time to familiarize ourselves with genetic research and its implications, we risk responding out of fear and ignorance and potentially discarding away crucial medical advances.

Genetic technology harbors great power for good and evil. We must work hard to take every thought captive to Christ and decide what is of benefit and what avenues of research and application must be avoided to preserve human freedom and dignity.

A genome is the complete set of instructions for making an organism. Thus, an individual's genome is the sum total of his or her genes. Each of the one hundred trillion cells in the human body contain tightly coiled and packed strands of a remarkable molecule called deoxyribonucleic acid (DNA), which are organized into chromosomes. If you laid out end to end the strands of DNA from all of our chromosomes in each of our cells, it would stretch six feet long. DNA is a polymer, a repetitive sequence of four bases (nucleotides), which I will refer to by their one-letter abbreviations: A, G, C, and T. The human genome sequence is simply the sequence in which these four bases appear in the DNA.

A gene is a specific segment of DNA that contains the precise coding sequence for a protein, and proteins do all of the real work in our cells, making up the structural components of cells and tissues. By looking at the completed genome sequence, experts predict that our genome consists of an estimated thirty thousand to forty-five thousand genes in each of our many trillions of cells.

What the Human Genome Project Hopes to Accomplish

So now that scientists have determined the sequence, what does that discovery mean? First, it is necessary to understand that, although the genome sequence as a whole has been discovered, researchers are still working to discover the sequence of ever smaller segments of DNA. The National Institutes of Health, in cooperation with several international research organizations, began HGP in 1990 in the United States. Among the many goals of HGP were four primary objectives.[1]

The first and primary objective was to map and sequence the entire human genome. A critical and significant difference exists between a map and the sequence. The human genome comprises more than three billion letters (see A, G, C, T above), spread out over twenty-three pairs of chromosomes. Locating a specific sequence of, say, one thousand letters, the number of which may code for a large protein, means locating that one sequence out of millions of such sequences. Therefore, researchers needed a refined road map to find their way through the total genome sequence. The genome map locates particular sequence markers that can be used like symbols on a road map. If a trait that a particular scientist is studying always seems to be present with this marker, the gene associated with the trait is probably nearby. In 1995, a detailed map was published with more than fifteen thousand markers, one for every two hundred thousand bases. This map would aid greatly in associating genes with particular diseases. And now, with the overall genome sequence complete and with more than 99 percent accuracy, determining the precise effect of a particular gene on a disease will be even easier.

A second objective was to map and sequence the genomes of several important model organisms, specifically the bacterium *E. coli*, yeast, roundworm, fruit fly, and mouse. Each of these organisms has for decades been used for laboratory studies. Being able to coordinate knowledge of their genomes with cellular and biological processes will even further inform the study of the human genome and its various functions.

A third objective of the HGP was to systematize and distribute the information it gathered. During the HGP's research, when any sequence of more than two thousand bases became mapped, the data was released within twenty-four hours. The sequence and map data are contained in publicly accessible databases on the Internet. HGP has also been creating software and other tools for large-scale DNA analysis.

A fourth goal of HGP is to study the ethical, legal, and social implications of genetic research. A full 5 percent of all funds appropriated for the HGP have been earmarked for such considerations. Many concerns revolve around the use of genetic sequence data, including worries about ownership, patenting, access to personal sequence data by insurance companies, potential for job discrimination based on personal sequence data, and the prospects for genetic screening, therapy, and engineering.

The Long-term Hopes for HGP

The completion of the genome sequence was jointly announced in February 2001 in the journals *Nature*[2] and *Science*.[3] Both journals have made these landmark issues available, without subscription, on their Web sites.

Recognizing the sequence of a particular gene has three important ramifications.[4] The first is diagnosis. Over the last few years, single genes have been found that lead to deafness and epilepsy. Most diseases, however, are influenced by a number of genes and in complex ways. Recently, genetic influences have been found in many forms of hypertension, diabetes, obesity, heart disease, and arteriosclerosis.[5] Genetic analysis of cancer tumors may someday help determine the most effective drug therapy with the fewest side effects. Genetic diagnosis may potentially lead to prescribing more precise treatments for many medical conditions.

Second, using genetics to more precisely diagnose ailments will lead to more reliable predictions about the course of a disease. Genetic information about an individual's cholesterol chemistry will aid in predicting the course of potential heart disease. Obtaining a genetic fingerprint of a cancerous tumor will provide information concerning its degree of malignancy. And more precise genetic information will also lead to the development of better strategies for prevention of disease.

Genetic information, too, can eventually be used to more specifically screen ailments in newborns, a procedure that may help avoid disorders later in life. Babies in the United States and other countries are currently screened routinely for PKU, a metabolic disorder that prevents the breakdown of a specific amino acid found in proteins. This condition becomes toxic to the nervous system but can be prevented and managed with appropriate diet. Without dietary changes, however, affected babies face extreme mental retardation. It is hoped that, through genetic technology, the number of conditions to which this type of screening applies can be expanded.

Screening can also be performed on adults to determine if they carry the potential for genetic conditions. Certain Jewish and Canadian populations regularly submit to voluntary screening for Tay-Sachs disease, a known child-killer. This information has been used to help make decisions about future marriage partners.

Perhaps the greatest benefit of the GNP will derive from what is called gene-based therapy. Understanding the molecular workings of genes and the proteins they encode will lead to more precise drug treatments. As stated above, the more precise the drug treatment, the fewer and milder will be the side effects.

Actual gene therapy—that is, replacing a defective gene with its normal counterpart—is still very experimental. Many hurdles remain, including how to deliver the gene to the proper cells, how to control where that gene is inserted into a chromosome, and how the gene is activated.

Does the Human Genome Sequence Vindicate Darwin?

It is not surprising that some people have seen the findings of the HGP as a vindication of Darwin. Amid the controversy and exultation over the HGP has been a not-so-quiet triumphal crowing from evolutionary biologists. The similarity of many genes across boundaries of species, the seemingly messy patchwork nature of the genome, and the presence of numerous apparently useless repetitive and copied sequences all have been argued as a clear validation of evolution.

Really? If Darwin were alive today, I suspect he would be astounded and humbled by what we now understand about the human genome and the genomes of other organisms. One bioethicist, however, Arthur Caplan, thought that the major news story was missed.[6] A few of his statements help us understand that little in his comments should be trusted. First, Caplan says, "Eric Lander of the Whitehead Institute in Cambridge, Massachusetts, said that if you look at our genome it is clear that evolution must make new genes from old parts."

Although we might be able to see some examples of shared sequences between genes, we can by no means see wholesale evidence of gene duplication throughout the genome. According to one group of researchers, less than four thousand of the thirty to forty-five thousand human genes share even 30 percent of their sequences with other genes.[7] More than twenty-five thousand genes—as much as 62 percent of the human genes mapped by the HGP— were unique (i.e., not likely the result of copying).

Second, Caplan says, "The core recipe of humanity carries clumps of genes that show we are descended from bacteria. There is no other way to explain the jerry-rigged nature of the genes that control key aspects of our development." Not everyone agrees. The complexity of the genome may reveal, rather than random jerry-rigging by evolution, intricate design. Because there is so much that we still do not know, Caplan speaks more out of ignorance and assumption than from data. Note the following comment by Gene Myers, one of the principal geneticists from Celera Genomics, from a story in the *San Francisco Chronicle:*

> "What really astounds me is the architecture of life," he said. "The system is extremely complex. It's like it was designed."
>
> My ears perked up. "Designed? Doesn't that imply a designer, an intelligence, something more

than the fortuitous bumping together of chemicals in the primordial slime?"

Myers thought before he replied. "There's a huge intelligence there. I don't see that as being unscientific. Others may, but not me."[8]

Jury-rigged genes? Hardly. Confusion at the moment about gene structure? Certainly. But more likely than messy jury-rigging will be revealed hidden levels of complexity. More than bluster is required to demonstrate that our genome is solely the result of evolution. The earmarks of design are clear—that is, if you have eyes to see.

Challenges of the Human Genome Project

Many people express concerns about the potential for abuse of genetic information. Although great potential exists for numerous positive uses of the human genome, many people fear unintended consequences for human freedom and dignity.

Some people are justifiably worried about the rush to patent human genes. The public consortium, through the National Institutes of Health, has made all of its information freely available and intends to patent nothing. But several patent requests on human genes are still pending from the time before HGP was completed.

It is important to realize that these patent applications are not necessarily for the genes themselves. Rather the patent protects the holder's right to priority to any products (e.g., therapies, drugs) derived from using the sequence in research. With the full genome sequence published, the answer of who has a right to what becomes even more muddled. No one is anxious for the courts to try its hand at settling the issue. Yet companies will need some level of protection as they develop new therapies based on genetic information, and at the same time it is important that public confidence be upheld and their health not compromised.

Another concern is the availability of information about individual genetic conditions. Some people worry that employers may use genetic information to practice discrimination in hiring or in deciding which current employees will be laid off or forced into retirement. Upward of 80 to 90 percent of Americans believe that their genetic information should be private and obtained or accessed only with their permission. Similar fears are expressed as to the legality of insurance companies using private genetic information to assess coverage and rates. A bill introduced in Congress (June 29, 2000) to address these very concerns was amended to the Health and Human Services appropriations bill, but it was removed in committee. The bill was to be reintroduced in the next session.[9] I would be very surprised if some level of privacy protection is not firmly in place by 2002.

Moreover, many people are apprehensive about the general speed of discovery and the very real possibility that genetic engineering will create a new class—the genetically enhanced.[10] Certainly, we have cause for vigilance. As previously stated, we can no longer afford to be ignorant of genetic technologies. And although the pace of progress could afford to slow down, neither should we throw out the baby with the bathwater.

After I delivered a series of lectures on genetic engineering and human cloning at a Christian high school, one student wrote the following message to me:

I am a senior, in an AP Biology class, and I find

genetics absolutely fascinating. It's both fascinating and scary at the same time. . . . [You have inspired me] to not be afraid of the world and science in particular, but to take on its challenge and trust God.

Amen to that!

Part 2

Trends in Society

Baby Boomerangs

Kerby Anderson

Baby boomers are returning to church! What do the stories and statistics associated with this trend signify? What do they mean? Is a spiritual revival taking place? What caused the original exodus from the church, and what is bringing about the return? This chapter addresses these and other questions.[1]

The baby boomers who are returning to church have been dubbed "baby boomerangs." Most of them grew up in religious households; about 96 percent had some religious instruction in their early years. But many jettisoned their religious beliefs when they became adults and—like boomerangs, returning to the point from which their flight began—they are now returning to church.

At least two processes were responsible for their exodus from organized religion. The process of secularization in modern society dislodged religious ideas and institutions from the dominant place they held in the minds of earlier generations. Religious ideas became less meaningful, religious institutions more marginal in their influence on the baby boom generation. To their parents' dismay, most boomers dropped out of traditional religion for at least two years during their adolescence and adulthood.

The second societal process, that of pluralization, rapidly multiplied the choices of worldviews, faiths, and ideologies. This increase in choice led naturally to a decrease in commitment and continuity. During their adolescence and early adulthood, many boomers went through what might be called serial conversions. Spiritually hungry for meaning, they dined heartily at America's cafeteria of alternative religions: est, gestalt, meditation, scientology, bioenergetics, and the New Age. Others sought spiritual peace through twelve-step programs for alcoholics, workaholics, even chocoholics.

This have-it-your-way, salad-bar spirituality has been high on choices and options but low on spiritual commitment. One author wrote, "Although there are those who try to follow the demanding precepts of traditional religion, most baby boomers find refreshment in a vague religiosity which does not interfere in any way with how they live."[2]

As the boom generation passes through midlife, it will inevitably look to the future more with anxiety than anticipation. Boomers are asking, "Who will care for me? Will I be able to provide for myself and my family?" These questions mingle with questions of identity. "Who am I? Where am I going? Is this all there is to life?" Such questions contain an underlying spiritual dimension and are not easily answered in either a secular world or a mystical world filled with bland spirituality.

Certainly, this generation has sought resolution for their spiritual needs in self-help programs and community activities, but social changes and technology have not held the answer. As one commentator said, "There is a feeling of being lost and looking for something greater. People know that technology hasn't worked for them. It hasn't done anything for their souls."[3]

This is, in part, why many baby boomers have begun to return to church. But does the return reflect a true spiritual revival? And a large segment of the boomer generation remains outside the church and is seemingly uninterested in coming back. What could the church do to reach out to them?

Seekers of Experiences

As in other endeavors, baby boomers have been seekers: seekers of pleasure, seekers of experience, seekers of freedom, seekers of wealth, and, yes, seekers of spirituality. But unlike their parents, as boomers sought spirituality they went down unpredictable paths. For boomers, brand loyalty is unheard of and the customer is king. Thus, they have been eclectic in their religious experience. Although some have stayed true to the faith of their fathers, most of them have sought a flexible and syncretistic mix of traditional religion, New Age mysticism, and modern self-help psychologies.

Tracking this generation's values in regard to, and attitudes toward, religion and spiritual issues is not easy, if for no other reason than the lack of substantial research. Most of the significant research on boomer attitudes toward religion have been done within the last ten years. Consider this comment from the late 1980s: "When the first of its number reached 40 last summer, the Baby Boom once again entered the spotlight. But for all the coverage, including a 10-page cover story in *Time* and [Landon] Jones' 350-page book, little more than a paragraph was written on the role of religion in the lives of the Baby Boom generation."[4] More research since then has provided a better perspective on boomer attitudes and their perspectives on religion.

Boomers can be divided into three religious subcultures: loyalists, returnees, and dropouts. Loyalists tend to be social conservatives. They maintained closer relations with their parents and tended to grow up in stricter homes. Loyalists never really identified with the counterculture and never left their church or synagogue.

At the other extreme are the dropouts. They had less confidence in the country when growing up and had more conflicts with their parents. Traditional religion was, to them, out of touch with modern life. They have never come back to church and pursue spirituality (if at all) personally and individually.

Between the loyalists and the dropouts are the returnees. They were—and are—middle of-the-road types who were less alienated than the dropouts but more disaffected than the loyalists. They left church or synagogue and have returned but often with some ambivalence.

Each religious subculture manifests differences in spiritual styles and commitment, but all of them are affected to some degree by their experiences in the counterculture. Although their views differ from one another, collectively the three boomer subcultures are very different from their parents. Few in the returnees subculture, for example, actually consider themselves religious and do not hold to traditional views of God, even though they might attend religious services regularly. Returnees are much less likely to engage in traditional religious activities (daily prayers, saying grace at meals, reading the Bible), and almost one-fourth of returnees and nearly one-fifth of loyalists say they believe in reincarnation.

In short, baby boomers are very different from their parents in terms of spiritual commitment and biblical understanding. And churches and Christian organizations, if they are to be effective in reaching out to boomers, must be aware of these differences.

"Teach Your Children Well . . ."

Those baby boomers who have returned to church—the so-called "baby boomerangs"—have returned for one of two major reasons: their children, or spiritual restlessness. Boomers who are concerned about the moral and spiritual upbringing of their children have made the spiritual pilgrimage back to their religious roots. Boomers may say that they do not believe in absolute values, but frequently their relativistic worldview collapses when they have children. They don't want their kids to grow up without any moral direction. Church suddenly becomes an important place. Gallup surveys show, for example, that nearly nine in ten Americans say they want religious training for their kids, even though fewer than seven in ten with children (ages 4–18) say that they are currently providing such training.

The boomerang phenomenon is not, however, peculiar solely to baby boomers. Church historians have found a predictable pattern of church attendance that has affected numerous generations. Typically, after high school, young adults drop out of church and often don't drop back into church until they have children. In that regard, boomers are no different than generations that preceded them.

Unlike previous generations, though, boomers prolonged the cycle by postponing marriage and children. Getting married later and having children later essentially extended the boomers' absence from church. And this extended absence allowed many of them to get more set in their ways. A generation used to having weekends free and sleeping in on Sunday is less likely to make church attendance a priority.

Kids begin to rearrange those priorities. Statistically, the presence of children in a family has been shown to make a significant difference in the likelihood of church attendance. One survey found that married baby boomers are nearly three times more likely to return to church if they have children. Children do, indeed, seem to be leading their parents back to church.

Another reason for boomers' return to church is spiritual restlessness. Sixteen hundred years ago, St. Augustine acknowledged, "We were made for thee, O God, and our hearts are restless until they find rest in thee."[5] Social commentators have generally underestimated the impact of the boomer generation's restless desire for meaning and significance.

Ken Woodward, religion editor for *Newsweek* magazine, believes "that search for meaning is a powerful motivation to return to the pews. In the throes of a midlife reevaluation, Ecclesiastes—'A time for everything under heaven'— is suddenly relevant."[6] George Gallup has found that two-thirds of those who dropped out of a traditional church (left for two years or more) returned because they "felt an inner need" to go back and rediscover their religious faith.[7]

For these and other less significant reasons, baby boomers are returning to church but not in the numbers that are sometimes reported in the media. All of this attention to returning boomers fails to take into account that more than 40 percent of baby boomers have *not* returned to church. And although many people are celebrating those coming in the front door, they shouldn't overlook the stream of boomers leaving the church out the back door. They are bored, disillusioned, or restless and must be reached more effectively if the church is to make a difference in the twenty-first century.

"If It Feels Good . . ."

Although much has been made of the baby boomerang phenomenon, many boomers are skeptical of church as well as other institutions such as government, military, and schools. Though boomers are consistent with previous generations in their boomerang cycle, "statistics on church attendance, when viewed up close, reveal dramatic and distinctive patterns along generational lines."[8] The data show the following:

- Throughout their lives, Americans born during the Depression have been more faithful than later generations in their church/synagogue attendance.
- "War babies" [born 1939–1945] dropped out of church as they entered their twenties during the turbulent sixties, and stayed away. The twin disillusionment stemming from Vietnam and Watergate made them more suspicious of institutions—the church included. Only recently, as they approach and pass midlife, are they trickling back to church.
- "Baby boomers" [born 1946–1964] also dropped out of the church in their twenties, but now, in their thirties and early forties, they are returning to the ranks of the faithful. The real boom in church attendance is coming from this generation.[9]

Boomers, then, are returning to church in increasing numbers. By the early 1980s the number of leading edge baby boomers who attended church regularly rose nearly 10 percent (33.5 percent to 42.8 percent) and continued to rise throughout the decade.

Will this revitalized interest in religion make a difference in society? This is a question that many social commentators are considering. Sociologist Os Guinness asks, "Will the churches and synagogues provide the kind of training necessary to keep the faith vital—or will the churches merely mirror the culture? . . . The natural tendency of the baby boomers is to be laissez-faire socially. Will their return to faith make any decisive difference in their personal and social ethics, or will their religious commitment be [simply] a variant of their social philosophy?"[10]

As stated, boomers have been samplers with little brand loyalty. They don't feel bound to the denomination of their youth, and they search for experiences (both spiritual and otherwise) that meet their needs. It is not uncommon for families to attend different churches each week (or on the same day) to meet their perceived spiritual needs. They aren't bashful about attending a particular church to take advantage of a special seminar or program and then picking up and moving to another church when the programs there seem inviting.

Many boomers might be interested in spiritual matters but see no need to attend church. George Gallup refers to this characteristic in his book *The Unchurched in America—Faith Without Fellowship*. Such religious individualism stems both from the American individualism that has been a part of this country for centuries and from this generation's desire for flexibility and individuality. The have-it-your-way expectation in every area of a boomer's life has given rise to this religious individualism.

Boomers approach religion and spirituality differently than did previous generations. They embrace a faith that is low on commitment and high on choice. As one commentator noted, "They are comfortable with a vague, elastic faith that expands to fill the world after a pleasant Christmas service and contracts to nothing when confronted with difficulties."[11] No wonder many boomers are starting to embrace religious beliefs that previous generations would never have considered.

Spiritual Hunger

Spiritually hungry boomers, looking for nourishment for their souls, have already tried a variety of selections from America's spiritual cafeteria. They will probably continue to do so. Lonely and isolated in suburban enclaves, often hundreds of miles from their families, boomers are facing significant psychological stress in the midst of busy lives that sap their emotional and spiritual resources. Beneath this isolation and turmoil is a restless desire for spirituality.

Some of them will try to meet these needs by dabbling in the New Age movement. And if the churches do not meet boomers' real and perceived needs, this trickle might turn into a torrent. The New Age movement is attractive to the spiritually naive and to those who are cynical toward traditional institutions. If the church fails, then the New Age will thrive.

Combating failure might, in fact, be the greatest challenge for the Christian church. Can church leaders woo baby boomers back to the flock? Can the church challenge boomers to a greater level of religious commitment in their lives? Can the church provide the religious training necessary to keep boomers' faith vital?

Churches must challenge boomers to deeper faith and greater religious commitment, but surveys and statistics show that churches themselves might be suffering from the same maladies as baby boomers. Church members like to believe that they are more spiritually committed and live lives that are different than those of the unchurched, but the data show otherwise.

Approximately 40 percent of America attends church or other religious services fairly regularly. But George Gallup has found that fewer than 10 percent of Americans are deeply committed Christians. Those who are committed "are a breed apart. They are more tolerant of people of diverse backgrounds. They are more involved in charitable activities. They are more involved in practical Christianity. They are absolutely committed to prayer."[12]

Numerous surveys show that most Americans who profess Christianity don't know the basic teachings of the faith. Such shallow spirituality makes them more susceptible to the latest fad, trend, or religious cult. Gallup notes that not being grounded in the faith means that they "are open for anything that comes along." Studies show, for example, that New Age beliefs "are just as strong among traditionally religious people as among those who are not traditionally religious."[13]

Lack of commitment to a faith position and to a lifestyle based upon biblical principles also extends to church attendance and instruction. Eight in ten Americans believe that they can arrive at their own religious views without the help of the church.

Nor is commitment to biblical instruction a high priority. George Gallup says that Americans are trying to do the impossible by "being Christians without the Bible." He adds, "We revere the Bible, but we don't read it."[14] Pastors and pollsters alike have been astounded by the level of biblical illiteracy in this nation.

Churches that reach out to baby boomers will have to shore up their own spiritual commitment as they challenge the boom generation to a higher level of commitment and discipleship. If churches are successful in doing so, then their congregations will grow; if they aren't successful, then boomers will go elsewhere to satisfy their spiritual hunger.

10

Generation X

Jerry Solomon

G*eneration X!* Are you familiar with that label? You've probably heard it or read it at least once. What does it bring to mind? Does it provoke fear, confusion, despair, and misunderstandings, or is it just another in a long line of such expressions used to label youth?

Generation X has quickly entered our vocabulary as an easily recognizable moniker for the children of another definable generation—the baby boomers. Most of the forty-one million generation Xers are children of the baby boomers, who number more than seventy-seven million. This dramatic decrease in the number of births from the boomer generation to the Xers has left the latter with the label *baby buster.* The terms *Xers* and *busters* normally don't elicit positive thoughts about our youth. Is this a legitimate response? Or are we maligning a significant portion of our population by attaching negative sounding labels?

In 1991, a Canadian named Douglas Coupland published a novel titled *Generation X: Tales for an Accelerated Culture.* Coupland's book "is the first major work to take twenty-somethings seriously, even if the book is humorous and fictional."[1] Thus, Coupland is the originator of the phrase that now describes a particular generation. But he is just one of many people who have thought about youth culture, both past and present.

A Brief History of American Youth

Youth seems always to have received the attention of adults. Teenagers, as they have come to be called, have been analyzed, diagnosed, and reprimanded because older generations just don't know what to make of them. *Juvenile delinquents*, *the beat generation*, *hippies*, *yuppies*, and numerous other titles have been used to describe certain generational distinctives. "The contemporary youth crisis is only the latest variation on centuries-old problems."[2] In the 1730s in New England, for example, youth activities such as "night 'walking' and 'company keeping,' also known as 'revels,' helped produce some of the highest premarital pregnancy rates in American history."[3] And during the early nineteenth century, student riots became a tradition on many campuses such as Brown, North Carolina, Princeton, Harvard, Yale, and Columbia. These riots included "boycotting classes, barricading college buildings, breaking windows, trashing the commons and/or chapel, setting fires around or to college buildings, beating faculty members, and whipping the president or trustees."[4] Such behavior—almost two hundred years ago—probably reminds us of what took place on many campuses during the Vietnam War years.

By the beginning of the twentieth century, youth became the focus of the burgeoning social sciences. "An intellectual enterprise struggled to redefine what 'youth' was or ought to be. That concept was labeled 'adolescence' and has prevailed ever since."[5] It is of special interest that these early social scientists didn't discover adolescence, they invented it. "Adolescence was essentially a conception of behavior imposed on youth, rather than an empirical assessment of the way in which young people behaved."[6]

That the concept of adolescence was an invention is significant when we understand that the worldview premises of the social scientists "came from Darwinian recapitulation theory: the individual life-course replicated the evolutionary progress of the entire race. Adolescence was a distinct 'stage' through which each person passed on the way from childhood (the 'primitive' stage) to adulthood (the 'civilized' stage). Adolescence therefore was transitional but essential, its traits dangerous but its labor vital for attaining maturity. Squelching it was just as bad as giving it free rein."[7] The fruit of such concepts can be seen in the "lifestyles" that are now so ingrained in our cultural fabric.

The Web of Adolescence

What do the "lifestyles" of adults have to do with adolescents? "Since 'lifestyle' has come to define not just doing but their very being, adults have now become dependent on the very psychological experts who wove the web of adolescence in the first place. The classic youth tasks of 'growth,' 'finding oneself,' and preparing for one's life-work have become the American life-work, even into the golden years' of retirement."[8] Thus, the concerns that we have for our youth are concerns that we have for ourselves. The "web of adolescence" touches all of us. As George Barna has stated, "Taking the time to have a positive impact [on our youth] is more than just 'worth the effort'; it is a vital responsibility of every adult and a contribution to the future of our own existence."[9] The importance of this point cannot be overemphasized as we contemplate the sometimes puzzling segment of our population called *Generation X*.

Who Are These People?

What is a Generation Xer or a baby buster? What is the "doofus generation" or "the nowhere generation"? These phrases, and many others, may be used to characterize the present generation of youth. They are not very encouraging phrases, are they? More frequently than not, adults always have evaluated youth in pessimistic terms. Even the ancient Greeks were frustrated with their youth.

Today, however, the descriptions are especially derogatory. "Words used to describe them have included: whiny, cynical, angry, perplexed, tuned out, timid, searching, vegged out—the latest lost generation."[10] Are these terms accurate, or do they reek of hyperbole? As is true with most generalizations of people, they include a measure of truth. But we make a grave mistake if we allow them to preclude us from a more complete consideration of generation Xers. As George Barna has written, "You cannot conduct serious research among teenagers these days without concluding that, contrary to popular assumptions, there is substance to these young people."[11]

Having served among and with youth for many years, I emphatically concur with Barna. As stated above, Generation Xers consist of "41 million Americans born between 1965 and 1976 plus the 3 million more in that age group who have immigrated here."[12] The "birth dearth" from the boomer generation to the Xers is the result of several social phenomena. At least six factors contributed to this population decline.

First, the U.S. experienced the world's highest divorce rate. Second, the use of birth control became increasingly prominent with the introduction of the pill. Women began to experience more freedom in planning their lives. Third, a college education was more accessible for more people, especially for women, who began to take more influential positions in the workforce. Fourth, social change, including women's liberation, encouraged more women to consider careers other than that of homemaker. Fifth, abortions reached a rate of more than 1.5 million per year. Sixth, the economy led many women to work because they had to, or because they were the sole bread-winner.[13]

So we can see that Generation X has entered a culture enmeshed in dramatic changes, especially regarding the family. These changes have produced certain characteristics—some positive, others negative—that are generally descriptive of contemporary youth.

How Do You Describe a "Buster"?

How do you describe someone who is labeled as a "baby buster"? We might be tempted to answer in a despairing tone, especially if we haven't taken time to see a clear picture of a "buster." Consider their characteristics:

1. They are serious about life. The quality of life issues they have inherited have, for example, challenged them to give consideration to critical decisions both for the present and future.
2. They are stressed out. School, family, peer pressure, sexuality, techno-stress, finances, crime, and even political correctness contribute to their stress.
3. They are self-reliant. One indicator of this concerns religious faith; the baby buster believes he or she alone can make sense of it.
4. They are skeptical, which is often a defense against disappointment.
5. They are highly spiritual. This doesn't mean they

are focusing on formal religion, but it does mean they realize that it is important to take spiritual understanding of some kind into daily life.

6. They are survivors. This is not apparent to adults who usually share a different worldview concerning progress and motivation. This generation is not "driven" as much as their predecessors. They are realistic, not idealistic.[14]

Do these characteristics match your perceptions? If not, it might be because Generation Xers have received little public attention. And what attention it has received has leaned toward the negative because of inaccurate observations. The baby busters' parents, the baby boomers, have been the focus of businesses, education, churches, and other institutions simply because of their massive numbers and their market potential. It's time to rectify these misperceptions and have the wisdom to foresee the impact that busters will have in the not-too-distant future.

What About the Church and Busters?

In an attempt to bring Generation X into sharper focus, a survey of their other attributes will be informative. These attributes should be especially important to those of us in the Christian community who desire to understand and relate to our youth.

Because of "the loneliness and alienation of splintered family attachments," this generation's strongest desires are acceptance and belonging.[15] Our churches need to become *accepting* places first and *expecting* places second. That is, our youth need to sense that they are not first *expected* to conform or perform. Rather, they are to sense that the church is a place where they can first find *acceptance*. One

of the consistent shortcomings of our churches is the proverbial "generation gap" that stubbornly *expects* youth to
dress a certain way, talk a certain way, socialize in a certain way, without *accepting* them in Christ's way.

Another important attribute of this generation is how
they learn. "They determine truth in a different way: not
rationally, but relationally,"[16] that is, "interaction is their
primary way of learning."[17] For the church to respond, it
might be necessary to do a great deal of "retooling" of the
way we teach.

Last, busters are seeking purpose and meaning in life.
This search culminates, of course, in a relationship with
the risen Jesus. Facilitating this relationship is the most
important contribution the church can offer. If we fail to
respond to the greatest need of this generation or of any
other, surely we should repent and seek the Lord's
guidance.

Listening to Busters

Let's eavesdrop on a conversation taking place on a college campus between a Generation X student and a pastor.

Pastor: We have a special gathering of college students
at our church each Sunday. It would be great
to see you there.

Student: No, thanks. I've been to things like that before. What's offered is too superficial. Besides,
I don't trust institutions like churches.

Pastor: Well, I think you'll find this to be different.

Student: Who's in charge?

Pastor: Usually it's me and a group of others from the
church.

Student: No students?

Pastor: Well, uh, no, not at the moment.

Student: How can you have a gathering for students and yet the students have nothing to do with what happens?

Pastor: That's a good question. I haven't really thought much about it.

Student: By the way, is there a good ethnic and cultural mix in the group?

Pastor: It's not as good as it could be.

Student: Why is that?

Pastor: I haven't really thought about that, either.

Student: Cliques. I've noticed that a lot of groups like yours are very "cliquish." Is that true at your church?

Pastor: We're trying to rid ourselves of that. But do you spend time with friends?

Student: Of course! But I don't put on a "show of acceptance."

Pastor: I appreciate that! We certainly don't want to do that! We sincerely want to share the truth with anyone.

Student: Truth? I don't think you can be so bold as to say there is any such thing.

Pastor: That's a good point. I can't claim truth, but Jesus can.

Student: I'm sure that's comforting for you, but it's too narrow for anyone to claim such a thing. We all choose our own paths.

Pastor: Jesus didn't have such a broad perspective.

Student: That may be, but he could have been wrong, you know. Look, I'm late for class. Maybe we can talk another time, as long as you'll listen and not preach to me.

Pastor: That sounds good. I'm here often. I'll look for you. Have a great day!

This fictitious encounter illustrates how baby busters challenge us to find ways of communicating that transcend what might have been the norm just a few years ago.

New Rules

George Barna has gleaned the following set of "rules" that define and direct youth of the mid- and late-nineties.

Rule #1: Personal relationships count. Institutions don't.

Rule #2: The process is more important than the product.

Rule #3: Aggressively pursue diversity among people.

Rule #4: Enjoying people and life opportunities is more important than productivity, profitability, or achievement.

Rule #5: Change is good.

Rule #6: The development of character is more crucial than achievement.

Rule #7: You can't always count on your family to be there for you, but it is your best hope for emotional support.

Rule #8: Each individual must assume responsibility for his or her own world.

Rule #9: Whenever necessary, gain control and use it wisely.

Rule #10: Don't waste time searching for absolutes. There are none.

Rule #11: One person can make a difference in the world but not much.

Rule #12: Life is hard and then we die; but because it's the only life we've got, we may as well endure it, enhance it, and enjoy it as best we can.

Rule #13: Spiritual truth may take many forms.

Rule #14: Express your rage.

Rule #15: Technology is our natural ally.[18]

Now let's consider how parents and other adults might best respond to these rules.

What Do They Hear from Us?

Try to put yourself into the mind and body of a contemporary teenager for a moment. Imagine that you've been asked to share the kinds of things you hear most often from your parents or adult leaders. Your list might sound something like this.

- "Do as I say, not as I do."
- "I'm the adult. I'm right."
- "Because I said so, that's why."
- "You want to be *what?*"
- "This room's a pigsty."
- "Can't you do anything right?"
- "Where did you find him?"
- "You did *what?*"
- "Do you mind if we talk about something else?"
- "I'm kind of busy right now. Could you come back later?"

These statements sound overwhelming when taken together. And yet many of our youth hear similar phrases too frequently. How might we better communicate with and minister to them?

Advice to Parents and Other Adults

In his book *Ten Mistakes Parents Make with Teenagers,* Jay Kesler shares advice for dealing with young people.[19]

1. Be a consistent model. We can't just preach to young people and expect them to follow our advice if we don't live what we say. Consistency is crucial in the eyes of a buster.

2. Admit when you are wrong. Just because you are the adult and the one with authority doesn't mean that you can use your position as a "cop-out" for mistakes. Youth will understand sincere repentance and will be encouraged to respond in kind.

3. Give honest answers to honest questions. Youth like to ask questions. We need to see this as a positive sign and respond honestly.

4. Let teenagers develop a personal identity. Too often, youth bear the brunt of their parents' expectations. In particular, parents will sometimes make the mistake of living through their children. Encourage them in their own legitimate endeavors.

5. Major on the majors and minor on the minors. In my experience, adults will concentrate on things like appearance to the detriment of character. Our youth need to know that we know what is truly important.

6. Communicate approval and acceptance. As we stated earlier in this essay, this generation is under too much stress. Let's make encouragement, not discouragement, our goal.

7. When possible, approve of your teens' friends. This advice can be especially difficult for many of us. Be sure to take time to go beyond the surface and really know their friends.

8. Give teens the right to fail. We can't protect them all of their lives. Remind them that they can learn from mistakes.
9. Discuss the uncomfortable. If young people don't sense that they can talk with you, they will seek someone else who might not share your convictions.
10. Spend time with your teens. Do the kinds of things they like to do. Give them your concentration. They'll never forget it.

This generation of youth, and all of those to come, need parents and adults who demonstrate the above qualities. When youth receive this kind of attention, our churches, our schools, our families, and our country will all benefit. And, most importantly, I believe that the Lord will be pleased.

The Spiritual Quest of Generation X

Rick Wade

If God had a name, what would it be?
And would you call it to His face?
If you were faced with Him in all His glory,
What would you ask if you had just one question?
Yeah, yeah, God is great.
Yeah, yeah, God is good.

God has made a comeback in pop music. In her song "One of Us," Joan Osborne wonders what we might ask God if we stood face-to-face with Him.[1] The music video for R.E.M.'s "Losing My Religion" shows a spilled pitcher of milk. Writer Tom Beaudoin sees that image as symbolizing the loss of religious authority in the lives of Gen-Xers.[2] Madonna's video for the song "Like a Prayer" is full of religious symbolism: an altar, a crucifix, candles, and other icons.[3]

Looking for God?

Tom Beaudoin, himself a member of Generation X, says that his generation is "strikingly religious." They express their spirituality through pop culture rather than through institutional religion.[4] The shift from the word *religion* to *spirituality* is significant. Having lost confidence that institutional religion can provide satisfactory answers, Xers look elsewhere, often mixing ideas and religious expressions from a variety of sources as each person chooses for himself or herself what to believe.

Beaudoin says that Xers are on an "irreverent spiritual quest." Feeling abandoned by parents, churches, politicians, and even technology, they seek their own paths in finding meaning for their lives. Campus minister Jimmy Long writes, "Xers are twice as likely as people in [the Boomer] generation to be children of divorce. Between 1960 and 1979 the American divorce rate tripled." He continues, "Fifty percent of today's teenagers are not living with both birth parents."[5]

Looking at circumstances outside the home, Xers feel let down as well, dismayed by the dilemmas that the boomer generation has left them.[6] Xers were alarmed, for example, by the TV movie *The Day After*, which was about the results of nuclear war. The spaceship *Challenger* blew up shortly after takeoff. Watergate was fresh in our cultural memory. Environmentalists point to the severe damage done to nature by technology. Xers see themselves as fixers, as those who have to clean up the mess that preceding generations made. But because their own backgrounds were often so difficult, many of them simply hope to take charge of their own lives.

Finding little stability around them, they lack confidence that such a thing as objective truth exists. Thus, having no ultimate truth by which they can make sense of everything, they feel the burden for providing their own meaning of life and for establishing their own moral standards. Long quotes Eric, a Gen-Xer who speaks of the stress that this situation puts on him: "There's too much pressure from outside," he says.

> Life gets pretty complicated when one has to think carefully about everything one does. Imagine that you had to decide for yourself whether a behavior is right or wrong. In the end, so many conflicts would be going on inside of you that you couldn't do anything; it becomes impossible to be happy with what you think at any point.[7]

That's what it's like for many Xers. And as a result, when they want to find their place in this world, they turn to friends. Their small communities of friends provide structures for truth and meaning. Consensus means more with respect to "truth" than do logic and facts.[8] "Busters process truth relationally rather than propositionally," say Celek and Zander.[9] The emphasis on community in Xer culture reveals their desire to get along, not get ahead, to connect, not conquer.[10]

Modernism's search for utopia without invoking God has been turned on its head with the Buster generation. Their horizons and ambitions might be smaller than those of their parents, but they have an openness to the transcendent that their parents didn't have. Spirituality is now an accepted aspect of life; Xers are open to a sense of fellowship with something bigger than themselves.

In Douglas Coupland's collection of short stories, *Life After God,* a man named Scout talks about himself and his small group of friends. He tells about the early, carefree days of fun and camaraderie, a time of living in a paradise in which "any discussion of transcendental ideas [was] pointless."[11] As time went by, however, they all saw their dreams fade in the realities of everyday life. Scout had this to say about his life:

> Sometimes I want to go to sleep and merge with the foggy world of dreams and not return to this, our real world. Sometimes I look back on my life and am surprised at the lack of kind things I have done. Sometimes I just feel that there must be another road that can be walked—away from this person I became—either against my will or by default. . . .
>
> Now—here is my secret:
>
> I tell it to you with the openness of heart that I doubt I shall ever achieve again, so I pray that you are in a quiet room as you hear these words. My secret is that I need God—that I am sick and can no longer make it alone. I need God to help me give, because I no longer seem to be capable of giving; to help me be kind, as I no longer seem capable of kindness; to help me love, as I seem beyond being able to love.[12]

This first fully postmodern generation must understand that they aren't alone: we *all* need God. The good news is that God has not left us wandering in a dark place but has come looking for us. He is not aloof, off making other worlds, or too busy gussying up heaven to notice us down here. He has taken on our flesh and become one of us. Joan Osborne asks, What if God was one of us? Well, He was! He looked like us, hurt like us, laughed like us. This chapter examines some of the characteristics of this God who became like us in order to show us that He has the answers to the Xers' need.

God: A Person Who Sees and Feels

If God had a face, what would it look like?
And would you want to see,
If seeing meant that you would have to believe,
In things like Heaven and in Jesus and the Saints,
And all the Prophets and . . .
Yeah, yeah, God is great.
Yeah, yeah, God is good.
Yeah, yeah, yeah, yeah, yeah.[13]

Joan Osborne wonders what God looks like. What *does* God look like? He doesn't have a physical body. But what does He "look" like in terms of character? Those of us who were born before Gen-X have a hard time understanding that many people in this generation have no real understanding of the God of the Bible, the One in whom we ask them to commit their very souls. Who *is* this God, anyway? Consider some of His characteristics.

A Person, Not a Force

First, God is a *Person,* not some Star Wars "force." Because we're created in His image we can learn some things about Him from looking at ourselves. Just as we are persons, He is a Person, too. "He possesses life, self-consciousness, freedom, purpose, intelligence, and emotion,"[14] just like we do. Thus, one could rightly say that the Old Testament patriarch Abraham could be called "the friend of God" (James 2:23). One cannot be a friend with a "force." Because God is a Person, He can be involved in our lives; a force cannot relate to us on a personal level.

One Who Sees . . .

Furthermore, this is a God who *sees*. The Bible teaches, "The eyes of the LORD are in every place, Watching the evil and the good" (Prov. 15:3). We're told that He knows completely. God knows when the sparrow falls from the sky; He even knows the number of hairs on our heads (Matt. 10:29–31)!

More importantly, God knows our hearts (Acts 1:24). This is great news to those who recognize their own need. But if it makes us fearful because we know the badness in our hearts, we're also told that "He knows how we are formed, he remembers that we are dust" (Ps. 103:14 NIV). God doesn't look for those who meet His standard; none of us can meet it. He looks for the one who will believe and then obey. In fact, at the place of our greatest need, He meets us.

. . . with a Father's Eyes

Beyond that, God presents Himself to us as a father, as *the* Father. Unlike many fathers today, God takes His fatherhood seriously. He provides for our needs (Matt. 7:11). Like a shepherd looking for a lost sheep, God looks for the one who strays away, not wishing that any should remain lost. In the New Testament there is a story about a father whose younger son asks for his inheritance, then squanders it on wild living. He winds up feeding pigs to earn his food. Finally, he comes to his senses and returns home, prepared to be as one of the hired men, to give up his rights as a son. As he approaches his home, his father sees him coming down the road. In his joy, the father gathers up his robe and runs down the road to embrace the son (and, in those days, men typically didn't act in such an undignified way), and he welcomes his son home. The father in the story represents God the Father.

One Who Feels

Even more than seeing, God *feels.* He truly "knows our pain." In Jesus, we see a God who weeps over the hardness of His people and who has compassion on those who are sick and those who are caught in sin. He knows the feeling of rejection, having been rejected even by those who were close to Him. When He was put to death by crucifixion, He felt the weight of sin although He had never sinned. And while bearing our sin, He felt forsaken by God, alienated, as it were, from His own Father.

In short, God is a Person who reveals Himself as the Father who knows all about us, as one who understands our hurts and who cares. This is a God who is in touch. This is a God to believe in.

The God Who Reaches Out

Loves and Cares

Scout says that he needs God. One reason, he says, is "to help me love, as I seem beyond being able to love."[15] The implication is, of course, that God has the capacity to help people love. To do this He Himself must be a God of love. The Bible says that God *is* love (1 John 4:8, 16). It is a part of His very *nature* to love, and this love is shown throughout Scripture in God's dealings with His people.

Some critics see God in the Old Testament as angry and vengeful. But they are selectively focusing on the actions of a just and holy God in His response to wrongdoing. They overlook the love of God poured out on His people as He cared for them, protected them, and provided for their needs. *Lovingkindness* is a word that is used many times in descriptions of God: "But you, O Lord, are a compassionate and gracious God, slow to anger, abounding in love and faithfulness" (Ps. 86:15 NIV).

This love isn't just for the elite, for "super people." God cares for the "regular people." "For there is no partiality with God" (Rom. 2:11; Acts 10:34). In fact he chastises His people for treating the influential differently than others (James 2:1–7) and for attending to all of their religious duties but not demonstrating true love to those in need. "Learn to do right!" He says. "Seek justice, encourage the oppressed. Defend the cause of the fatherless, plead the case of the widow" (Isa. 1:17 NIV). The second greatest commandment, in fact, is to love our neighbor as ourselves (Luke 10:27–37), and our neighbor is *anyone* who is in need. Jesus reached out to the outsiders—the prostitutes, the lepers, and the poor. Those who recognized their problems were the ones most drawn to Him.

Identifying and Drawing Near

What this reveals is a God who doesn't stand aloof but who instead draws near. From the beginning of the human race, He has been reaching out to us. When the first people sinned, God took the initiative to repair the breech. He established the people of Israel, and constantly sought after them, even when they were in open rebellion. Such care was a precursor to God's most astonishing move. His love for us was so great that He chose to become one of us. He didn't stay apart from us; rather, He identified with us in the person of Jesus of Nazareth. Although he was God, He emptied Himself, was "made in human likeness," and became a servant (Phil. 2:7 NIV).

As the shepherd searches for his sheep, God came looking for us. "Being in very nature God," the Bible says, Jesus "did not consider equality with God something to be grasped, but made himself nothing, taking the very nature of a servant, being made in human likeness. And being found in appearance as a man, he humbled himself and became obedient to death—even death on a cross!" (Phil. 2:6–8 NIV). In Jesus, God became a man so that He could bring humankind to Him. And He did it by becoming one of us. This is a God to believe in.

The God Who Receives, Redeems, Reconciles, and Restores

Receives

A problem of many Gen-Xers is the feeling that they aren't acceptable. As stated earlier, half of today's teens live with only one parent, and a child perceives the departure of a parent through divorce as a personal rejection. Such familial rejection, whether real or perceived, colors a child's attitude about himself or herself and his or her acceptability. Many Gen-Xers feel shame, thinking that they aren't good enough. "If Dad or Mom left," they think, "I must not be worth much."

Even in cases where both parents were present, children were often left to raise themselves because of their parents' jobs. "They were the first full-blown 'latchkey children,'" say Celek and Zander, "coming home to a house where nobody was home."[16] What might at first seem like wonderful freedom often resulted in fear and a sense of aloneness. Even day care wasn't always enough to relieve the sense of being alone. Being left with strangers, even kind and well-meaning strangers, felt like abandonment to many kids.

God isn't like fallen people, however. He receives anyone who will come to Him. He never turns anyone away, and He never leaves. We need not fear enemies from without, difficult tasks ahead, or the lack of provision for our needs (Deut. 31:6; Josh. 1:5; Heb. 13:5). "I will never fail you or forsake you," is His promise, a promise that has been affirmed by His people for centuries.

Redeems

The value that God places on us is evinced by Jesus' death on the cross. By His death He *redeemed* us; He bought us out of slavery to make us children of God. We are no longer "owned" by our old way of life. The slave standing on the block has been bought and paid for—not to remain a slave but to become a child of the Redeemer. The price that we couldn't pay, Jesus did.

Reconciles

Because of their feelings of rejection Gen-Xers can have problems getting close to people. After all, for many of them, even their parents were aloof; why should they get close to others? They might not feel that they *can* get close to others.

We're told in the book of Romans that God has taken the initiative to bring us close to Him, to reconcile us to Him. Whereas formerly we were alienated from Him, now we can come near to Him in open communication. "We have peace with God through our Lord Jesus Christ," the apostle Paul wrote (Rom. 5:1). God breaks down the walls for us.

Restores

Once our sin is taken care of through faith in Christ and we are reconciled with God, we begin the process of being restored in the image of Christ. A fundamental change occurs in us when our spirits are made alive through

Christ. Building upon that change, the Spirit of God begins slowly changing us from the inside out, conforming us to the image of Jesus, and making us like Him. This restoration will be complete when we are with Him.

Summarized in the Cross and the Resurrection

This entire process—God's receiving, redeeming, reconciling, and restoring us—is summed up in the work of Jesus on the cross. He paid the ultimate price for us and enabled us to be reconciled to the Father. And in His death He called all people to Himself (John 12:32). Furthermore, when He rose from the grave, restored to life never to die again, He revealed to us what our hope is: our own resurrection revealing our full restoration in His image. This restoration begins here on earth through the work of God's Spirit in us. It will be made complete when we are raised up, never to die again.

In the life, death, and resurrection of Jesus, we see God receiving, redeeming, reconciling, and restoring. God has done the work. This is a God to believe in.

The God Who Can Be Trusted

If the people who are the most important to you have lied to you, wouldn't you become distrustful? David Hocking tells of a woman who had been put into a special institution after her parents had divorced. Her parents rarely visited. When she was old enough to be on her own, she began wandering from town to town, experiencing abuse and broken promises. As a result, she didn't trust anyone. Reverend Hocking says, "As I began telling her of God's love for her, she asked, 'Can He be trusted?' I answered, 'Of course. He's God!' She countered, 'Why should I trust Him? Everyone else has let me down!'"[17]

What does it take to build trust in a person? Hocking gives three elements: telling the truth, doing what is right and fair, and being reliable. Do these characteristics describe God?

Tells the Truth

Because God is holy, or separate, from all that is sinful, He is morally pure. As such, He cannot lie. "It is *impossible* for God to lie," says the New Testament (Heb. 6:18 emphasis added). If He says that He will do something, He will do it (Num. 23:19). The people of Israel discovered that God was true to His word in fulfilling His promises. He gave them the land that He had promised them, and when they turned away from Him, He spared them repeatedly because of the covenant that He had made with their forefathers. And because God cannot lie, those who believe in Him can rest in the promise of His constant presence and in the promise of eternity with Him (Titus 1:2; Matt. 28:20).

Does What Is Right and Fair

We also can count on God to do what is fair or just. If He couldn't be depended upon to do that, we would have no reason to trust Him. What if He arbitrarily changed the rules on us and judged us by a different standard? A student complains that his teacher grades inconsistently. She seems to be arbitrary in assigning values to projects, and often gives no clear word on what she expects. The student says that she isn't being fair. A boss shows favoritism among his employees, advancing those who are his friends while leaving the truly worthy employees behind. Not fair, we say.

God is not like that. He plays straight. He tells us what

He expects, and He shows no partiality in His judgments. "Righteous are You, O LORD," says the psalmist, "and your laws are right" (Ps. 119:137 NIV). Likewise, He demands justice of us: "Blessed are those who maintain justice, who constantly do what is right" (Ps. 106:3 NIV).

Can Be Depended Upon

Finally, God can be counted on. He is faithful to His Word and His character. Knowing what He is like teaches us what He does. And one of His characteristics is being always the same: "For I, the LORD, do not change," He says (Mal. 3:6). He is the one "who does not change like shifting shadows" (James 1:17 NIV). God is faithful forever to His own nature.

He is also faithful to His decrees and His promises. "I foretold the former things long ago, my mouth announced them and I made them known," He said. "[T]hen suddenly I acted, and they came to pass" (Isa. 48:3 NIV). He promised Sarah a child in her old age, and He gave her one (Gen. 21:1). King Solomon said, "Not one word has failed of all the good promises he gave through his servant Moses" (1 Kings 8:56 NIV).

God can be trusted. He tells the truth, He does what is fair, and He can be counted on. To Generation X, to those of all generations, this is a God you can believe in.

12

Time and Busyness

Kerby Anderson

I t's always been true—time is money. But for the current generation this maxim has a new twist. As with any commodity, the law of supply and demand determines value. And in the last two decades, free time has become even more scarce than money; therefore, it has become more valuable.

We live in the age of time famine. Leisure time, once plentiful and elastic, is now scarce and elusive. People seeking the good life are finding that enjoying it—even if they can afford it—has become increasingly difficult. According to a Lou Harris survey, the amount of leisure time enjoyed by the average American has shrunk 37 percent since 1973. A major reason is an expanding workweek. Over this same period, the average workweek (including commuting) has increased from fewer than forty-one hours to nearly forty-seven hours.[1] And in many professions— such as medicine, law, and accounting—an eighty-hour week is not uncommon. Harris concludes that "time may have become the most precious commodity in the land."[2]

The Technology of Time

Our current time crunch has caught most people off guard. Optimists in the 1950s and 1960s, with visions of

Utopia dancing in their heads, predicted that Americans would enjoy ample hours of leisure by the turn of the century. Computers, satellites, and robotics would remove the menial aspects of labor and deliver abundant opportunities for rest and recreation.

The optimists were partly right: computers crunch data at unimaginable speeds, orbiting satellites transmit over the globe a dizzying array of messages, and robots zap together everything from cars to computer chips at speeds far exceeding the capabilities of humans. Yet these and other technological feats have not freed Americans from their labors. Most people are busier than ever.

It wasn't supposed to be this way. Testimony before a Senate subcommittee in 1967 predicted that "by 1985, people could be working just 22 hours a week or 27 weeks a year or could retire at 38."[3] The major challenge in the 1990s should have been what to do with all the leisure time that our technological wizardry provided. Instead, technology has been more of an enemy than an ally. "Technology is increasing the heartbeat," says Manhattan architect James Trunzo, who designs automated environments. "We are inundated with information. The mind can't handle it all. The pace is so fast now, I sometimes feel like a gunfighter dodging bullets."[4]

The problem isn't so much technology, though; it's the heightened expectations that it engenders. The increased speed and efficiency of appliances, computers, and other machines have enabled us to accomplish much more than was possible in previous decades. But this efficiency has also fostered a desire to take on additional responsibilities and thereby squeeze even more activities into already crammed calendars.

As the pace of our lives has increased, overcommitment

and busyness have been elevated to socially desirable standards. Being busy is chic and trendy. Pity the poor person who has an organized life and a livable schedule. Everyone, it seems, is running out of time.

Time-Controlling Devices

It's little wonder that most of the products now being developed are not so much time-savers as time-controllers. Most of the appliances developed in the 1950s—vacuum cleaners, dishwashers, mixers—were designed to save time and remove drudgery from housework. By comparison, most of the products developed in the last few decades— VCRs, answering machines, automatic tellers—are time-controllers. These devices do not save much time, but they do allow harried consumers to use their time more effectively.

Technological efficiency has also increased competition. Baby boomers compete intensely with one another for jobs and prestigious promotions, avidly employing the latest equipment to give them an edge. They view labor-saving devices that are supposed to make life easier—faxes, car phones, laptop computers—as necessities that let them work harder and remain competitive.

But technology itself isn't enough to maintain the competitive edge. Most professionals—especially those in service industries such as law, accounting, and advertising—work long hours in an effort to meet their clients' seemingly endless needs and demands. Other baby boomers feel trapped in the rat race, believing that economic pressures make it impossible to support a family on one income.

The work ethic seems out of control. In the frenetic dash for success or just plain survival, leisure time becomes a scarce commodity. "My wife and I were sitting on the beach in Anguilla on one of our rare vacations," recalls James Trunzo, "and even there my staff was able to reach me. There are times when our lives are clearly leading us."[5]

No Time to Talk

People everywhere seem to be overscheduled and over-committed. Workers are weary. Parents are preoccupied. And children and family relationships are often neglected.

A recent survey by Cynthia Langham at the University of Detroit found that parents and children spend only four-teen and a half minutes per day talking to each other.[6] That's less time than a football quarter and certainly much less time than most people spend commuting to work. Langham says that many people are shocked to hear the fourteen-and-a-half-minute statistic. But once they apply a stopwatch to their conversations, they realize that she's right.

And even that fourteen-and-a-half-minute statistic is misleading; most of that time is squandered on chitchat such as, "What's for supper?" and "Have you finished your homework?" Truly meaningful communication between parent and child occupies only about two minutes each day. Langham concludes, "Nothing indicates that parent-child communications are improving. If things are chang-ing, it's for the worse."[7]

She points to two major reasons for this communica-tion breakdown. First is a change in the workforce. A few decades ago, the dinner table was a forum for family busi-ness and communication. But now, when dinnertime rolls around, Dad is still at work, Mom is headed for a business meeting, and Sister has to eat and run to make it to her part-time job. Even when everyone is home, meaningful communication is constantly interrupted.

The second reason for poor parent-child communication is the greatest interruption of all: television. Urie Bronfenbrenner of Cornell has reported a forty-year decline in the amount of time children spend with their parents, and much of the recent loss is due to television. Television sabotages much of the already-limited time that families spend together. Meals are frequently eaten in front of the "electronic fireplace." After dinner, talk-starved families gather to watch congenial television families, such as the Huxtables on the Cosby show, who have good communication skills. True, some television shows deal with issues that families might discuss (drugs, pregnancy, honesty), but few families take advantage of these program as an opportunity to provide moral instruction.

The greeting card business has developed a whole new product line for busy parents and children. More and more children are finding cards in their backpacks or under their pillows that proclaim, "Have a good day at school," or lament, "I wish I were there to tuck you in."

The effect of time pressures on the family has been devastating. Yale psychology professor Edward Ziglar somberly warns that "as a society, we're at the breaking point as far as family is concerned."[8] Homemaking and child rearing are full-time activities. When both husband and wife work outside the home, maintaining a household and raising a family becomes difficult. In the increasing numbers of single-parent households, the task becomes next to impossible. Someone has to drive carpools, make lunches, do laundry, cope with sick kids and broken appliances, and pay the bills. In progressive homes, household tasks are shared as the traditional husband/wife division of labor breaks down. In others, Supermom is expected to step into the gap and perform flawlessly.

Inevitably, children are forced to grow up quickly and take on responsibilities that they should never have to shoulder. Some children are effectively abandoned—if not physically, at least emotionally—and must grow up on their own. Others are latchkey kids who are forced to mature emotionally beyond their years. These demands take their toll and create what sociologist David Elkind has called the "hurried child" syndrome.[9]

Time—or rather our lack of it—is severely hurting families. Nurturing suffers when families don't have the time to communicate and parents don't have the time to instruct their children. In the end, lack of time takes its toll on the stability of families.

Never Enough Time

A 1989 survey by *Family Circle* documented the loss of time in families, especially for mothers who work outside the home. The article was titled "Never Enough Time?" and began, "Remember 'quality time'? In the 1980's that was what you sandwiched in for the children between the office and the housework. We all learned how valuable time was in the school of hard knocks. Life was what happened while we were busy making other plans, to paraphrase ex-Beatle John Lennon." That was then.[10]

A resounding 71 percent of all women surveyed said that their lives had gotten busier in the previous year.[11] Nearly a third attributed this increase in busyness to expanding workloads on the job, the demands of new employment, or the pressures of starting a business or returning to work. Not only do women work longer hours but many of them work on weekends, and nearly a third of them often take work home.[12]

Dual-income couples reported major difficulties

finding time for each other. Negotiating schedules and juggling calendars were daily activities. Three out of four women in the survey reported that finding enough time to be alone with their husbands was "often" or "sometimes" a major stress in their relationships.[13] When asked, "In a time crunch, who gets put on the back burner?" half said friends, then husbands, and then other family members.

Those hit hardest by time pressures were single parents. One Illinois single mother with two teenagers wrote, "I am responsible for a house and yard, work forty hours a week, take college classes, run a local support group for divorced and widowed women, and am involved with a retreat group through church. I have time because I *make* time."[14]

When time is in short supply, the first thing women will often let slide is housekeeping. A full 82 percent said that they had changed their standards of cleaning and organizing a house. When asked why, 49 percent said that other things were more important, 42 percent said that they were more relaxed about letting chores wait, 35 percent said that they had one or more young children, and 23 percent said that they had taken a paying job.

Organization expert Stephanie Winston says that the young generation of working women has reframed expectations about household responsibilities. She says, "Their sense of what is expected of them is really very different from what was expected ten years ago, when women joining the workforce had been raised on the old model— rearing the family, cooking, cleaning and the proverbial white-glove test." But whether they were in the workforce or full-time homemakers, more than half of the women surveyed were either "very" or "somewhat" dissatisfied with the amount of time that they have just for themselves. Only 30 percent try to set aside four or more hours a week just for themselves. Another 30 percent carve out two to three hours. But 19 percent say that they give themselves an hour or less a week, and 20 percent do not allot themselves any leisure time at all.

The time pressure on women and families is significant, squeezing out meaningful communication and important time to think and reflect. Gaining authentic "quality" time will not come without changes in our lifestyles.

Redeeming the Time

Time—or the lack of it—will continue to dominate our thinking in the twenty-first century. All of us are in the midst of a time crunch; the solution is to recognize our priorities and apply them rigorously.

First, we must establish biblical priorities in our lives. Often, our busyness is merely a symptom of a deeper problem, such as materialism. In Luke 12, Jesus illustrated this with the parable of the rich fool. He says, "The land of a certain rich man was very productive. And he began reasoning to himself, saying, 'What shall I do, since I have no place to store my crops?' And he said, 'This is what I will do: I will tear down my barns and build larger ones, and there I will store all my grain and my goods. And I will say to my soul, "Soul, you have many goods laid up for many years to come; take your ease, eat, drink and be merry."' But God said to him, 'You fool! This very night your soul is required of you; and now who will own what you have prepared?'" (Luke 12:16–20).

We can derive a number of applications from this passage. First, are we so involved in the affairs of the world that we neglect the affairs of the spirit? To reverse the familiar adage, we can be so earthly minded that we are no heavenly good.

Second, are we abandoning productive resources for a more luxurious lifestyle. If a three-bedroom house is sufficient, are we selling it merely to move up to a four-bedroom house? If the car we are currently driving is fine, are we nevertheless eager to trade it in on a newer or more expensive model? Often, our indulgences strain our time and financial resources.

This observation leads to our second biblical principle: fight materialism in our lives. Proverbs 28:20 says, "He who makes haste to be rich will not go unpunished." Materialism brings with it a haste to get rich. Materialistic people are not patient people. They always want something more—and they want it now! Often, our lack of time is tied to our haste to get rich, to feed our greed. We must ask ourselves, "How much do we really need?" If we fight materialism and cut back on the lavishness of our lifestyles, we might be surprised at how much time becomes available.

A third biblical principle is to redeem the time. Ephesians 5:15–16 says, "Therefore be careful how you walk, not as unwise men, but as wise, making the most of your time, because the days are evil." Colossians 4:5 says, "Walk in wisdom toward [outsiders], redeeming the time" (KJV).

What, though, does it mean to "redeem the time"? Unlike many of the other resources that God has given us, time is not renewable. We might lose money, but we can always earn more. We might lose our possessions, but we can always acquire new ones. But time is a nonrenewable commodity. If we squander our time, it is lost forever.

Yes, setting aside time for oneself is a legitimate use of the resource. But so is spending time with family, with friends, on volunteer work, to show kindness to strangers, in worship. The key to spending time wisely is balance. All of us, but especially Christians, must carefully balance the time that God has given us. We can either devote it all to acquiring possessions and public admiration or redeem it as a spiritual investment.

We can spend it only once, however, and how we spend it can have eternal consequences. Let us not waste the resources that God has given us. Instead, let us redeem the time and use it for God's glory.

13

Loneliness

Kerby Anderson

The baby boom generation is headed for a crisis of loneliness. The reasons are simple: demographics and social isolation. More boomers are living alone than in previous generations, and those who are living with another person will still feel nagging pangs of loneliness.

In previous centuries, when extended families dominated the social landscape, it would be unthinkable for a sizable proportion of adults to live alone. And even in the twentieth century, adults who lived alone usually were near the beginning (singles) and the end (widows) of adult life. But these periods of living alone are now longer because of lifestyle choices on the front end and advances in modern medicine on the back end. Baby boomers are postponing marriage and thus extending the number of years that they are single. Moreover, people are living longer, thereby increasing the number of years that one adult will be living alone.

Yet, the increase in the number of adults living alone is owing to more than just the changes stated above. Increasing numbers of boomers are living most or all of their adult lives alone. In the 1950s, only one in every ten households had one person in them, and those people were primarily widows. But today, as a result of the three *D*s of social statistics (death, divorce, and deferred marriage), about one in every four households consists of a single person. If current trends continue, sociologists predict that the ratio will increase to one in every three households by early in the twenty-first century.

In the past, gender differences were significant in determining the number of adults living alone. Young people in single households were, for example, more likely to be men because women tended to marry younger than did men. On the other hand, old people in single households were more likely to be women because women lived longer than did men. Although these trends still hold true, the gender distinctions are blurring as boomers of both sexes reject the traditional attitudes toward marriage. In contrast to their parents, boomers are marrying less, marrying later, and staying married for shorter periods of time.

Marriage Patterns

The most marriageable generation in history has not made the trip to the altar in the same percentages as their parents. In 1946, the parents of the baby boom set an all-time record of 2,291,000 marriages. This record was not broken during the late 1960s and early 1970s, when millions of boomers entered the marriage-prone years. Finally, in 1979, the record that had lasted thirty-three years was finally broken when the baby boomers achieved 2,317,000 marriages.

Nonetheless, many boomers, instead of marrying, chose to merely "live together." When the baby boom generation entered the traditional years of marriageability, the number of unmarried couples living together in the United States doubled to well over a million in just ten years. The sharpest change was among cohabiting couples under twenty-five years of age, who increased ninefold after 1970. Demographers estimate that as many as one-and-a-half to two million couples in the United States have cohabited. Yet even these high figures underestimate the lifestyle changes of boomers. These figures represent merely the number of couples living together at any one time. Cohabitation is a fluid state, so the total number living together or living alone is in the millions.

The boomer generation not only married less but also married later. Until the baby boom generation arrived on the scene, the median age of marriage remained stable. But since the mid-fifties, the median age of first marriages has been edging upward. Now both men and women are marrying a full eighteen months later than their counter parts of a generation earlier.[1]

The boomers, too, *stayed* married less than did their parents. The baby boom generation has the highest divorce rate of any generation in history. And they divorce not only more often but earlier in their marriages. When the divorce rate shot up in the sixties and seventies, the increase did not come from empty nesters who finally filed for divorce after sending their children into the world. Instead, it came from young couples divorcing before they even had children. Demographer Tobert Michael of Stanford calculated that whereas men and women in their twenties comprised only about 20 percent of the population, they contributed 60 percent of the growth in the divorce rate in the sixties and early seventies.[2] Taken together, these statistics point to a coming crisis of loneliness for the boom generation. More and more middle-aged adults will find themselves living alone.

Thomas Exeter, writing in *American Demographics,* predicts, "The most dramatic growth in single-person households should occur among those aged 45 to 64, as baby boomers become middle-aged."[3] These households are expected to increase by 42 percent, and the number of men living alone seems to be growing faster than the number of women living alone.

The crisis of loneliness will affect more than just the increasing number of baby boomers living alone. Although the increase in the number of adults living alone is staggering and unprecedented, these numbers are fractional in contrast to the number of baby boomers who are in relationships that leave them feeling very much alone.

Commitment—the "C" word, as it was often called in the eighties—is a significant issue. It is a foreign concept to most of the million-plus cohabiting couples. These arrangements are often transitory, forming and dissolving with alarming frequency. Many people cohabit out of convenience, demonstrating little of the commitment that is necessary to make a relationship work. Anyone who is looking for intimacy and commitment will not likely find them by cohabiting.

Commitment is sometimes lacking, too, in marriages. Spawned in the streams of sexual freedom and multiple lifestyle options, boomer marriages seem less permanent, and couples appear less committed to making marriage work than were previous generations. Marriages, which are supposed to be the source of stability and intimacy, often produce uncertainty and isolation.

Living-Together Loneliness

Psychologist and best-selling author Dan Kiley has coined the term *living-together loneliness*, or LTL, to describe this phenomenon. He has estimated that ten to twenty million people (primarily women) experience LTL.[4]

Living-together loneliness is an affliction of the individual, not the relationship, although that may be troubled, too. Kiley believes that LTL is the effect of two primary causes: the changing roles of men and women and the crisis of expectations. In the last few decades, especially following the rise of the modern feminist movement, expectations between the sexes have been altered significantly. When these expectations do not match reality, disappointment (and eventually loneliness) sets in.

Kiley first noted this phenomenon in 1970 among his female patients. He came to realize that loneliness occurs in two varieties. The first type is the loneliness felt by single, shy people who have no friends. The second type is more subtle because it strikes people who are in a relationship but who nevertheless feel isolated and very much alone.

According to Kiley, "There is nothing in any diagnostic or statistical manual about this [feeling]. I found out about it by listening to people."[5] Kiley discovered that some men have similar feelings, but the typical LTL sufferer is a woman between the ages of thirty-three and forty-six who is married and living a comfortable life. She might have children. She blames her husband or live-in partner for her loneliness. Often, he's critical, demanding, and uncommunicative. The typical LTL woman realizes that she's becoming obsessed with her bitterness and is often in counseling for depression or anxiety. She is frequently isolated and feels some estrangement from other people, even close friends. Sometimes, she will have a fantasy about her partner's dying, believing that her loneliness will end if that man is out of her life.

To determine if a woman is experiencing LTL, Kiley employs a variation of an "uncoupled loneliness" scale devised by researchers at the University of California at Los Angeles. For example, an LTL woman would agree with the following propositions: (1) I can't turn to him when I feel bad; (2) I feel left out of his life; (3) I feel isolated from him, even when he's in the same room; (4) I am unhappy being shut off from him; (5) no one really knows me well.

Kiley also documents five identifiable stages of LTL that are likely to affect baby boom women. A typical LTL woman who marries at about age twenty-two will feel bewildered until she is twenty-eight. At that point, isolation sets in. At thirty-four, she begins to feel agitated. This turns to depression between the ages of forty-three and fifty. After that, a woman faces absolute exhaustion.

Women may soon find that loneliness has become a part of their lives whether they are living alone or "in a relationship," because loneliness is more a state of mind than it is a social situation. People who find themselves trapped in a relationship may be more lonely than a person who is living alone. Resolving that loneliness depends upon whether that person reaches out and develops strong relationship bonds.

Male Loneliness

In recent years, social psychologists have expressed concern about the friendless male. Many studies have concluded that women have better relational skills, which help them to be more successful at making and keeping friends. Women, for example, are more likely than men to express their emotions and display empathy and compassion in response to the emotions of others. Men, on the other hand, are frequently more isolated and competitive and, therefore, have fewer (if any) close friends.

Men may not, in fact, be conscious of their loneliness and isolation. In his book *The Hazards of Being Male: The Myth of Masculine Privilege,* Herb Goldberg asked adult men if they had any close friends. Most of them seemed surprised by the question and usually responded, "No, why? Should I?"[6]

David Smith lists in his book *Men Without Friends* the following six male characteristics that prove to be barriers to friendship.[7] First, men have an aversion to showing or expressing emotions. At a young age, boys receive the cultural message that they are to be strong and stoic, and as men, they shun emotions. Such an aversion makes deep relationships difficult, inhibiting men from making and keeping friendships.

Second, men seemingly have an inherent inability to fellowship. In fact, men find it hard to accept the fact that they need fellowship. If someone suggests lunch, it is often followed by the response, "Sure, what's up?" Men may get together for business, sports, or recreation (hunting and fishing), but they rarely do so just to enjoy each other's company. Centering a meeting around an activity is not bad, it is just that the conversation often never moves beyond work or sports to deeper levels.

Third, men have inadequate role models. The male macho image prevents strong friendships because a mask of aggressiveness and strength keeps men from knowing themselves and others.

Fourth, men are competitive. Men think that they must excel in what they do. Yet this male competitive spirit is frequently a barrier to friendship.

Fifth, men seem to have an inability to ask for help, perceiving it as a sign of weakness. Some others simply don't want to burden their families or colleagues with their problems. In the end, male attempts at self-sufficiency rob them of fulfilling relationships.

Sixth, men often have a distorted sense of priorities that values physical things above relationships. Success and status is determined by material wealth rather than by the number of close friends.

Men tend to limit their friendships and thus their own identity. H. Norman Wright warns,

> The more a man centers his identity in just one phase of his life—such as vocation, family, or career—the more vulnerable he is to threats against his identity and the more prone he is to experience a personal crisis. A man who has limited sources of identity is potentially the most fragile. Men need to broaden their basis for identity. They need to see themselves in several roles rather than just a teacher, just a salesman, just a handsome, strong male, just a husband.[8]

Crowded Loneliness

Loneliness, it turns out, is not just a problem of the individual. Loneliness is endemic to our modern, urban society. In rural communities, although the farmhouses are far apart, community is usually very strong. Yet, in our urban and suburban communities today, people are physically very close to each other but emotionally very distant from each other. Thus, close proximity does not translate into close community.

Dr. Roberta Hestenes at Eastern College has coined the term *crowded loneliness* to describe this type of social isolation. She says,

Today we are seeing the breakdown of natural "community" network groups in neighborhoods like relatives, PTA, etc. At the same time, we have relationships with so many people. Twenty percent of the American population moves each year. If they think they are moving, they won't put down roots. People don't know how to reach out and touch people. This combination produces crowded loneliness.[9]

Another reason for social isolation is the American desire for privacy. Although many boomers desire community and long for a greater intimacy with other members of their generation, they will choose privacy even if it means a nagging loneliness. Ralph Keyes, in his book *We the Lonely People,* says that above all else Americans value mobility, privacy, and convenience.[10] These three values make developing a sense of community almost impossible. In his book *A Nation of Strangers,* Vance Packard argued that the mobility of American society contributed to social isolation and loneliness. He describes five forms of uprooting that were creating greater distances between people:[11]

- First is the uprooting of people who move again and again. An old Carole King song asks the question, "Doesn't anybody stay in one place any more?" At the time Packard wrote the book, he estimated that the average American would move about fourteen times in his or her lifetime. By contrast, he estimated that the average Japanese would move five times.
- The second is the uprooting that occurs when communities undergo upheaval. The accelerated

population growth during the baby boom, along with urban renewal and flight to the suburbs, has been disruptive to previously stable communities.

- Third, a type of uprooting occurs as the result of housing changes within communities. The proliferation of multiple-dwelling units in urban areas crowds together people who frequently live side by side in anonymity.

- Fourth is the increasing isolation due to work schedules. When continuous-operation plants and offices dominate an area's economy, neighbors remain strangers.

- And fifth is the accelerating fragmentation of the family. The steady rise in the number of broken families and the segmentation of the older population from the younger heightens social isolation. In a very real sense, a crisis in relationships precipitates a crisis in loneliness.

Taken together, the contributors to loneliness discussed in this chapter paint a chilling picture of the beginning of the twenty-first century. But they also present a strategic opportunity for the church. Loneliness will be on the increase in this decade, and Christians have an opportunity to minister to people cut off from normal, healthy relationships.

The local church should provide opportunities for outreach and fellowship in their communities. Individual Christians must reach out to lonely people and become their friends. Ultimately, we must help a lost, lonely world realize that their best friend of all is Jesus Christ.

14

Midlife Transition

Kerby Anderson

E ach year, four million baby boomers turn forty. Nothing is magical about turning forty per se, but for many, turning forty often signals a time of transition, a time of introspection and reevaluation. And, over the next few decades, millions of people will encounter that midlife transition. Why does this transition occur? How does it affect people? And how can Christians marshal the emotional and spiritual resources to deal with the resulting changes? These and other questions will be addressed in this chapter.

During the late 1980s and 1990s the first wave of the baby boom generation hit the midlife transition. Born in the late 1940s and early 1950s, many lived in new houses built on new streets in new neighborhoods in the new American communities known as the suburbs.

When they headed off to school they, in general, sat in new desks and were taught about Dick and Jane by teachers fresh out of college. They grew up with television and lived in a world brimming with promise. In the 1960s, they graduated from high school and enrolled in college in record numbers. Then they flooded the job market, many landing jobs at good salaries in a still-expanding economy and bought homes before housing prices and interest rates went through the roof.

Unlike many baby boomers who were born after them, the leading edge achieved, in large part, the American dream. They weren't necessarily smarter or more talented. Their success was in part the result of their having been born earlier. Of those who achieved a degree of financial success, however, many began to encounter a crisis. They are like the cartoon that appeared in *The New Yorker.*[1] A husband turns to his wife at the breakfast table and says, "The egg timer is pinging. The toaster is popping. The coffeepot is perking. Is this it, Alice? Is this the great American dream?"

Millions of people in the baby boom generation will no doubt repeat these questions in the next few decades. Is this it? Is this the great American dream? Add to these questions others: Where is my life going? Is this all I am ever going to achieve?

In some ways, these are strange questions coming from the leading-edge boomers who enjoy the fruits of the American economy. They have achieved a measure of success, yet they are asking questions that signal a coming crisis of purpose.

Why this crisis of purpose? And why now?

The Age Forty Transition

As they enter midlife, the baby boomers remain an enigma. Its members often rejected the values of their parents and changed the structure of their families in ways that were unimaginable to a previous generation. But they must now shoulder adult responsibilities and assume positions of leadership (if they aren't already in them). Put another way, the baby boom generation stands at a point of transition.

This is not the first time that this generation has collectively faced a point of transition. When the leading-edge boomers began turning thirty, they hit what psychologist Daniel Levinson calls the "Age 30 Transition."[2] Although their early to late twenties saw, in general, economic good times, the struggle of leaving childhood and entering adulthood was worked out in a period of stagnant wages and appreciating house prices. Ultimately, the collective angst of the boom generation turned Gail Sheehy's book *Passages: Predictable Crises of Adult Life* into a runaway best-seller.[3] Among other things, the book assured the baby boomers that they were not alone in their confrontation with a major life stage.

A large segment of the boomer generation is now in the midst of a more significant transition: the midlife transition. Turning forty is no more a predictor of change than was turning thirty. But somewhere in one's forties, midlife reevaluation begins. Men and women evaluate and question their priorities, their dreams, and their aspirations.

Although this transition is both somber and serious, some people have attempted to inject some levity into the discussion. Lawyer Ron Katz found the YUPPIE designation an inaccurate description of his friends' lifestyles. So he coined, somewhat facetiously, yet another acronym to describe boomers at this stage. No longer rolling stones, but not yet the grateful dead, they're MOSS—middle-age, overstressed, semiaffluent suburbanites.[4]

According to Katz, MOSS (or MOSSY, if you prefer the adjective) is what YUPPIES have become in the 1990s. As Katz says, a MOSS is "41 years old; more overstressed than overworked; affluent but doesn't feel that way."[5] A MOSS also is beginning to understand why the world hasn't changed more over the past twenty-five years, and he or she hopes that the world changes somewhat less over the next thirty years.

Although some social commentators want to discount the existence of an actual crisis, psychologists and sociologists assure us that something indeed happens at midlife. But in actuality, the transition to midlife is gradual. No major landmarks or signposts signal our entry into this area that for each individual is new and uncharted. Perhaps so many jokes exist about turning forty because one's fortieth birthday provides a visible demarcation of a gradual process.

The Seasons of Life

In the preface of his book *The Seasons of a Man's Life,* Daniel Levinson says, "Adults hope that life begins at 40—but the great anxiety is that it ends there."[6] Fearing that this may be true, many baby boomers are becoming "frantic at forty-something." They are making, without any hope or optimism, a transition from the years of their youth to a time of adulthood.

In his book, Levinson describes a number of developmental stages in adult life. He delineates an early adult era from the mid-twenties to the late thirties. He also discusses a middle adult era from the mid-forties to the early sixties. The years in between he calls the years of midlife transition. He sees these years as a bridge between young adulthood and senior membership in one's occupational world.

The psychological study done by Levinson focused on men between the ages of thirty-five and forty-five. He found that about 80 percent of those studied went through a time of personal crisis and reevaluation during this midlife transition. Levinson argued that the 20 percent who did not experience a struggle were in a state of denial and would go through this transition later. This argument raises the first of two assumptions that reside in these studies.

Although the stages and themes documented by these studies are descriptive, they are by no means normative. As a Christian, I reject a deterministic model that predicts that everyone will go through a certain stage. While writing an earlier book on the subject of death and dying, I found that not all people go through the same psychological stages of grief. Christians who have come to terms with their own mortality and the mortality of their loved ones can face death and agree with the apostle Paul that it is better "to be absent from the body, and to be present with the Lord" (2 Cor. 5:8 KJV). Likewise, people who have come to grips with their place in the world might not face a wrenching midlife crisis.

A second assumption relates to the subjects of those studies. The major studies of adult development (including Levinson's study) used male subjects born before the Great Depression. Comparable studies were not conducted for women or for baby boomers.

The men in the study have at least three things in common: they grew up in stable families, they had realistic goals for their lives, and they became adults in an expanding economy. Few of them experienced divorces in their families. Most of them had simple goals such as "being able to provide for their families" and "being a good father." They also built their careers in a flourishing economic climate.

These assumptions are not true for the baby boom generation. They grew up in families that were less stable and are now raising families in a world where divorce is very common. Baby boomers have much greater expectations and thus have personal goals that are much more difficult to attain. And baby boomers reached adulthood when the economy was shrinking.

The differences between the world the boomers grew up in and that of their parents make it difficult to apply Levinson's studies directly to the boom generation. Although some investigators claim the argument for a true midlife "crisis" is overblown, most of them believe that the current generation will be even more susceptible to a crisis than was the previous generation.

New Roles

In his research, Levinson discovered a number of themes that surface during the time of midlife transition. The first is that midlife transition involves adapting to new roles and responsibilities. By the time we (note that Levinson's studies involved only men) are in our thirties, we're expected to think and behave like a parent. We can postpone this role for a while, and the boom generation has been fairly successful at postponing adulthood by simply extending the period called *youth*. Boomers extended adolescence into their twenties and even into their thirties. Now they're facing different and more demanding sets of roles and expectations. They are taking senior positions in their jobs, and they must provide care for both their children and their aging parents.

A man in his forties is usually regarded by people in their twenties as a full generation removed. He is perceived more as a parent than as a sibling. In the minds of those who are younger, he is "Dad" rather than "buddy." This message comes first as a surprise and then as an irritation to a man in midlife.[7]

Another way to look at life transitions is based upon the work of Spanish philosopher José Ortega y Gasset. He identifies five generations: childhood, youth, initiation, dominance, and old age.[8]

The initiation generation includes the time of midlife transition and leads to what Gasset calls the dominant generation, during which individuals are expected to assume the mantle of leadership, authority, and responsibility. According to Gasset, the initiation and dominant generations are the two most crucial periods. The relations between these generations and the successful passing of authority from one to the other affect the fate of society. The transition from the current older generation to the younger generation will take place during the early part of the twenty-first century.

Mortality

The second stage of midlife transition involves dealing with one's own mortality. In midlife, we become increasingly aware of death. Living in a death-denying culture shields us from a sense of our own mortality. And being young further heightens our sense of indestructibility. As teenagers and young adults we think of ourselves as "bulletproof" and immortal. But by the age of forty, we have seen many people not much older than we succumb to cancer and heart attacks. Many of us have seen death in our own families. The death of a parent is a clear signal that we are now on our own. It also reminds us how short life really is.

People going through this transition face not only a crisis of mortality but also a crisis of growing old. Baby boomers are entering what I call the "ache age." Vigorous exercise is followed by aching muscles that seem to stay sore longer. Cuts and bruises that used to heal almost overnight now take much longer to heal. Such physiological reminders also focus our attention on our own mortality.

The five stages of grief identified by Dr. Elisabeth Kübler-Ross—although describing the psychological stages of a patient who is dying—correlate remarkably well with the feelings that people experience in midlife. Whether mourning the death of an individual or the death of one's dreams, the emotions are often the same.

Culminating Events

A midlife transition surfaces from a culminating event. This event serves as a marker for the conclusion of young adulthood. It might be a very obvious event such as being promoted or being fired from a job. But it also might be something that no one else would be able to identify, not even our spouses. It is a milestone that helps us see that one of our life's dreams is not going to be realized, and it provides an estimate for future success or fulfillment.

In *The Seasons of a Man's Life,* Daniel Levinson argues that the dreams we have are so compelling that nothing short of total success will satisfy us. In other words, there is no such thing as modest success. The culminating event is frequently seen as evidence of flawed success and often as total failure.

To those on the outside looking in, a person might seem to have reached the pinnacle of success. But they can't see into that person's irrational mind, which is affected by sin. He or she might have dreams that are hopelessly unrealistic, especially in youth.

It might be that a man is the president of a very successful company, but nevertheless he feels like a failure because his dream was to be the president of the United States. A man who is very athletic and runs marathons feels unfulfilled because his dream was to play in the NBA. A woman who is one of the top salespeople in the company might feel inadequate because she wanted a family and cannot have kids.

Intense Introspection

Fourth, midlife transition involves intense introspection. A consistent pattern of adult life is a struggle in early adulthood to achieve a measure of success followed by a midlife appraisal of one's values and philosophy of life. Levinson found that a man around forty begins to reassess the meaning of life and to reconsider the fate of his youthful dreams. He asks major questions: Is this all I am going to do the rest of my life? Is this all I am going to achieve?

Many people find that what they thought was going to make them happy isn't making them happy. They enjoyed law school and the first few years of law, but the thought of practicing law for the rest of their lives is not very fulfilling. They enjoyed the first few years selling life insurance, but the thought of selling insurance for another thirty years sounds more like torture than a career.

This is a time when an individual shines a light on his or her accomplishments and sets an agenda for the second half of life. Depending on the evaluation, that person might or might not make major midcourse corrections.

Leaving a Legacy

Finally, a midlife transition involves leaving a legacy. As we come to grips with our own mortality, we inevitably desire immortality, which is "one of the strongest and least malleable of human motives."[9] Leaving a legacy means finding a form of immortality by leaving something behind. One is reminded of Woody Allen's quip that he didn't want to be immortal by leaving something behind; he wanted to be immortal by not dying. But because that is not possible, then an individual seeks to leave a legacy, and that quest usually forms the core of the second half of a person's life.

Successful resolution of midlife comes from determining what legacy—possessions, memories, ministry—we will leave behind. The legacy might encompass family, work, or all of society. It might involve contributions as a parent, spouse, leader, or mentor. These elements of the legacy define the path we will take in the second half of our lives.

Application

These, then, are the basic themes of the midlife transition. For the Christian, two points of application can be made. First is a personal application. If you are going through midlife, recognize that you are going to be in a daily battle over three areas. First, you will have a daily battle with your thoughts. You need to take "every thought captive to the obedience of Christ" (2 Cor. 10:5). You will also have a daily battle with temptation. A key verse to memorize is 1 Corinthians 10:13 (NIV) ("No temptation has seized you except what is common to man . . ."). And finally, you will have a daily battle with sin and must confess your sins (1 John 1:8–9).

The second application relates to Christians as the body of Christ, and concerns personal ministry. If we are attentive to this midlife transition we, meaning the whole church body, will be able to minister to millions of people who will go through this struggle. These early years of the twenty-first century might be the greatest time for harvest in this generation. Until now, most baby boomers have had few struggles. As they confront midlife, however, many of them will be asking important questions that can lead to evangelistic opportunities.

Here are two ways you can help, both relating to knowledge. Daniel Levinson says that knowing the transition is coming is an important antidote to its effects. So a knowledge of this transition can help you to reach out and help others through their struggle.

Second, a knowledge of the Bible can help you minister. The members of a generation that has been impervious to the gospel might be more willing to listen as they ask the fundamental questions of life. If we reach out in love with a biblical message, we can make a difference.

15

Sex and Violence on Television

Kerby Anderson

I t should be self-evident. The sex and violence portrayed on television has gotten worse. In the past few years, the number of portrayals has increased and the images are more graphic. But I talk to many people who contend that television programming is not much different than it was just a few years ago. This chapter addresses sexual and violent images on television, and argues that programming has indeed deteriorated.

On March 30, 2000, the Parents Television Council issued a special report entitled *What a Difference a Decade Makes.*[1] The study compares prime-time sex, language, and violence in 1989 to that of 1999. It's not surprising that the report found a steady and, in most cases, sharp decline in broadcast television that is acceptable for family viewing. Following are a few of the findings:

- First, on a per-hour basis, sexual material was more than three times as frequent in 1999 as it was in 1989. The report gives many examples of how the sexual language on television has changed dramatically within just one decade. Most of the language is too graphic to represent here. The report also found that references to homosexuality increased dramatically. Whereas references to homosexuality were rare in 1989, they were mainstream in 1999, becoming more than twenty-four times as common during the decade. Homosexual characters and homosexual dialogue, once taboo, are now standard fare on many network television programs.

- Second, the study found that the rate of foul language in 1999 was more than five and one-half times higher than that of 1989. The report provides examples of the kinds of words and phrases that are routinely used but, again, they are not appropriate for me to list in this article.

- Third, the study found that violent incidents occurred at about the same rate in both years, but the intensity of those incidents greatly increased. Some of the programs reviewed showed nothing but violent images. So in terms of sexual content, coarse language, and violent material combined, the per-hour figure almost tripled from 1989 to 1999.

In every area of measurement the council found that sex, language, and violence increased dramatically in the last decade. Although this finding is not surprising, it does provide the best quantifiable measure of what has been taking place on television. No longer can defenders of television say that TV is "not that bad." The evidence is in, and television is more offensive than ever. Our perception that television has gotten worse is not just perception; it's reality.

Television's Impact on Behavior

Despite television fare's becoming worse in the last ten years, some defenders of programming argue that the impact of such programs is minimal. Again, the work of the Parents Television Council is helpful. They cite various studies and surveys that document the effects of television, especially on young people.

Looking at the impact that violent programs have on behavior, the Parents Television Council cites a review of nearly one thousand studies presented to the American College of Forensic Psychiatry in 1998. They found "that all but 18 [studies] demonstrated that screen violence leads to real violence, and 12 of those 18 [studies] were funded by the television industry. In 1992, the American Psychological Association concluded that 40 years of research on the link between TV violence and real-life violence has been ignored, stating that the 'scientific debate is over' and calling for federal policy to protect society."[2]

Less research has been conducted on the effect of other offensive television content on other behavior. Nevertheless, substantial evidence can be cited that the sexuality and language of young people are also significantly affected by television. Professional organizations such as the American Academy of Pediatrics have drawn links between television's depictions of sexuality and real-life behaviors.[3]

A 1995 poll of children ten to sixteen years of age revealed that children recognize that "what they see on television encourages them to take part in sexual activity too soon, to show disrespect for their parents, [and] to lie and to engage in aggressive behavior." More than two-thirds said that they are influenced by television; 77 percent said that TV shows too much sex before marriage, and 62 percent said that sex on television and in movies influences their peers to have sexual relations when they are too young. Two-thirds also cited certain programs featuring dysfunctional families as encouraging disrespect toward parents.

The report reminds us that television sets the baseline standard for the entire entertainment industry. Most homes (98 percent) have a television set, and the average household watches seven hours, fifteen minutes of television daily.[4] Other forms of entertainment (movies, videos, CDs, the Internet) must be sought out and purchased. Television is universally available and thus has the most profound effect on our culture.

As Christians, we must be aware of these cultural influences on us and our families. But we should also be concerned about the impact that television and other forms of media have on our neighbors and our society as a whole.

Sexual Content on Television

Most Americans believe that television programming is too sexually oriented. A survey conducted in 1994 found that 75 percent of Americans thought that television had "too much sexually explicit material." Moreover, 86 percent believed that television had contributed to "a decline in values."[5] And no wonder. Scanning the ads for movies or channel surfing through the television reveals plots celebrating premarital sex, adultery, and even homosexuality. As the documentation stated earlier, portrayals of sexual promiscuity on television are at an all-time high.

A previous chapter dealing with pornography discussed the dangers of becoming involved with sexually explicit materials, especially when it is linked with violence.[6] Neil Malamuth and Edward Donnerstein document the volatile impact of sex and violence portrayed in the media. They say, "There can be relatively long-term, anti-social effects of movies that portray sexual violence as having positive consequences."[7]

In a message given by Donnerstein, he concluded with this warning and observation: "If you take normal males and expose them to graphic violence against women in R-rated films, the research doesn't show that they'll commit acts of violence against women. It doesn't say they will go out and commit rape. But it does demonstrate that they become less sensitized to violence against women, they have less sympathy for rape victims, and their perceptions and attitudes and values about violence change."[8]

It is important to remember that these studies are applicable to not just hard-core pornography. Many of the studies used films that are readily shown on television (especially cable television) any night of the week. And many of the movies shown today in theaters are much more explicit than those shown just a few years ago.

Social commentator Irving Kristol asked this question in a *Wall Street Journal* column: "Can anyone really believe that soft porn in our Hollywood movies, hard porn in our cable movies and violent porn in our 'rap' music is without effect? Here the average, overall impact is quite discernible to the naked eye. And at the margin, the effects, in terms most notably of illegitimacy and rape, are shockingly visible."[9]

Christians must be careful that sexual images on television don't conform them to the world (Rom. 12:2). Instead, we should use discernment. Philippians 4:8 (NIV) says, "Finally, brothers, whatever is true, whatever is noble, whatever is right, whatever is pure, whatever is lovely, whatever is admirable—if anything is excellent or praiseworthy—think about such things."

The number of sexual situations seen on television is at an

all-time high, so we as Christians must exercise care in screening what we and our families see. And because the negative images seen on television affect all of society, we are justified in being concerned about the images that not only we see but those our neighbors see on television as well.

Violence on Television

Children's greatest exposure to violence comes from television. TV shows, movies edited for television, and video games expose young children to a level of violence unimaginable just a few years ago. The American Psychological Association says that the average child watches eight thousand televised murders and one hundred thousand acts of violence before finishing elementary school.[10] That number more than doubles by the time that child reaches age eighteen.

At a very young age, children are seeing a level of violence and mayhem that in the past might have been seen only by a few police officers and military personnel. Television daily brings hitting, kicking, stabbing, shootings, and dismemberment right into our homes.

The impact on behavior is predictable. Two prominent Surgeon General reports in the last two decades link violence on television to aggressive behavior in children and teenagers. In addition, the National Institute of Mental Health issued a ninety-four page report, *Television and Behavior: Ten Years of Scientific Progress and Implications for the Eighties*, that revealed "overwhelming" scientific evidence that "excessive" violence on television spills over into the playground and the streets.[11] In one five-year study of 732 children, "several kinds of aggression, conflicts with parents, fighting and delinquency, were all positively correlated with the total amount of television viewing."[12]

Long-term studies are even more disturbing. University of Illinois psychologist Leonard Eron studied children at age eight and then again at eighteen. He found that television habits established at the age of eight influenced aggressive behavior throughout childhood and adolescent years. The more violent the programs viewed by eight-year-old boys, the more aggressive their behavior, both at age eight and ten years later. He concluded that "the effect of television violence on aggression is cumulative."[13]

Twenty years later, Eron and Rowell Huesmann found that the pattern continued. He and his researchers found that children who watched significant amounts of TV violence at the age of eight were consistently more likely to commit violent crimes or engage in child or spouse abuse at thirty.[14] They concluded "that heavy exposure to televised violence is one of the causes of aggressive behavior, crime and violence in society. Television violence affects youngsters of all ages, of both genders, at all socioeconomic levels and all levels of intelligence."[15]

As was discussed earlier, nearly one thousand studies were presented to the American College of Forensic Psychiatry in 1998 that documented some of the effects described here. Violent images on television affect children adversely, and Christians do well to be concerned about the impact.

Psychological and Spiritual Implications

Television is such a part of our lives that we often are unaware of its subtle and insidious influence. As previously stated, 98 percent of homes have a television set, so we tend to take it for granted and are often oblivious to its influence.

Many people have told me that they watch television,

and that it has no impact at all on their worldview or behavior. But the Bible teaches that "as [a man] thinks in his heart, so is he" (Prov. 23:7 NKJV). What we view and what we think about affects our actions. And there is abundant psychological evidence that television viewing affects our worldview.

George Gerbner and Larry Gross, working at the Annenberg School of Communications in the 1970s, found that persons who engage in a great deal of television viewing—persons known as "heavy viewers"—live in a scary world. "We have found that people who watch a lot of TV see the real world as more dangerous and frightening than those who watch very little. Heavy viewers are less trustful of their fellow citizens, and more fearful of the real world."[16] They defined heavy viewers as those adults who watch an average of four or more hours of television a day. Approximately one-third of all American adults fit that category.

Gerbner and Gross found that violence on prime-time TV exaggerated heavy viewers' fears about the threat of danger in the real world. Heavy viewers, for example, were less likely to trust others than were light viewers. Heavy viewers also tended to overestimate their likelihood of being involved in a violent crime.

And if this finding is true of adults, imagine how television violence affects children's perceptions of the world. Gerbner and Gross say, "Imagine spending six hours a day at the local movie house when you were twelve years old. No parent would have permitted it. Yet, in our sample of children, nearly half the twelve-year-olds watch an average of six or more hours of television per day."[17] Thus, a large portion of young people fit into the category of heavy viewers. Their view of the world cannot help but be profoundly shaped by TV. Gerbner and Gross conclude, "If adults can be so accepting of the reality of television, imagine its effect on children. By the time the average American child reaches public school, he has already spent several years in an electronic nursery school."[18]

Television viewing affects both adults and children in subtle ways. We must not ignore the growing body of data that suggests that the images we see on that box in our living rooms does affect our perceptions and behaviors. Our worldview and our actions stemming therefrom are affected by what we see. Christians, therefore, must be careful not to let television conform them to the world (Rom. 12:2). We should, instead, develop a Christian worldview that is outside the box.

16

Kids Killing Kids

Kerby Anderson

All kids have problems. Used to be, though, a kid's biggest problem was getting a flat tire on a bike or having a mean teacher assign homework over the weekend. How times have changed. Who'd have guessed that one of the perennial news stories would be kids killing kids?

This chapter discusses school shootings and, more broadly, kids killing kids. Why is it happening? What can be done to stem the tide of violence on campus and in society? Such contributors as video games, teenage rebellion, and tolerance will be examined, as will the spiritual implications of children becoming violent.

Gunshots on a high school campus remind us that our world has changed. The body count of students and teachers makes us wonder, "What's going on?" In some cases, the shooters are teenagers with elaborate plans and evil desires. But sometimes the hail of bullets comes from impulsive kids as young as eleven years old.

In the past, if and when we talked about kids killing kids, the violence took place in an urban setting. Gangland battles between the Bloods and the Crips reminded us that life in the inner city was hard and ruthless. But the latest battlegrounds have not been Watts, the Bronx, or Cabrini-Green. These violent confrontations have taken place in rural, idyllic towns with names like Pearl, Mississippi; Paducah, Kentucky; Jonesboro, Arkansas; Littleton, Colorado.

We are shocked and surprised. Newspapers display the faces of kids caught up in the occult, and we wonder how they were attracted to such evil. The faces seem like Opie and Beaver look-alikes who have been charged with five counts of murder, and we wonder if they even understood what they were doing.

The answers from pundits have been many. Young people are desensitized to violence, and they learn to kill by using point-and-shoot video games. Teenagers are rebellious, and they are looking for a way to defy authority. In the past, that was easier to accomplish; one merely violated the dress code. Today, in a society that values tolerance, coming up with behavior that is intolerable is getting harder and harder to do. And the social and spiritual climate in which our kids live is hardly conducive to moral living.

Kids killing kids is the best evidence yet of a culture in chaos, a culture that has turned its back on God's moral law. Do we really believe that children can see thousands of TV murders or play violent computer games and not be tempted to act out that violence in real life? Do we think that we can lower societal standards and not have kids act out in bizarre ways? Do we think that we can pull God from the schools and prayer from the classroom and see no difference in the behavior of children? Kids killing kids is evidence of a nation in moral free fall.

The Media and Video Games

Do the media and video games influence the behavior of young people? Other chapters have addressed the impact of violent media on our society. We shouldn't be surprised that such violence is having a negative effect on our kids.

Lieutenant Col. Dave Grossman knows this truth only too well. He is a retired West Point psychology professor, Army Ranger, and an expert in the study of violence and killing in war. He is also an instructor at Arkansas State University in Jonesboro, Arkansas, and was one of the first people on the scene of the Jonesboro shootings. He has a lot to say.

He saw the devastation wrought by the shootings—and not just the five dead and ten wounded. He saw what happens when violence intrudes into everyday life. And he sees where the violence comes from. Says Grossman, "Anywhere television appears, fifteen years later, the murder rate doubles."[1]

He adds, "In the video games, in the movies, on the television, the one behavior that is consistently depicted in glamorous terms and consistently rewarded is killing." Grossman believes that media violence was a significant factor in the killings in Pearl, Mississippi; in West Paducah, Kentucky; in Jonesboro, Arkansas; in Springfield, Oregon; in Littleton, Colorado.

He also says that the combination of a sense of inferiority and the exposure to violence can provoke violence in young boys who are "wanna-bes." Sometimes they see violence as a route to fame, and one has to wonder whether all of the media exposure of these school shootings will spawn even more such violence.

Consider the 1995 movie *The Basketball Diaries.* In the film, Leonardo DiCaprio (also of *Titanic* fame) goes into a schoolroom and shoots numerous children and teachers. In doing so, he became a role model for young boys who are "wanna-bes."

The parents of three students killed in Paducah, Kentucky, have brought a lawsuit against the company that distributed the film *The Basketball Diaries.* The parents' lawyer points out that Michael Carneal, who opened fire on a group of students in Kentucky, viewed the film and honed his shooting skills by playing computer games such as *Doom* and *Redneck Rampage.*

Dave Grossman goes into some detail in showing how violence in the media—films, videos, and television—can affect us. The examples in his book *(On Killing: The Psychological Cost of Learning to Kill in War and Society)*[2] parallel the content in the media today—and the parallels are chilling. Two factors in effecting violent behavior are desensitization and operant conditioning. Show soldiers (or children) enough visual images of violence, and they will become desensitized to it. Practice shooting targets of people and conditioning will eventually take over when shooting at the real thing. In some ways, it doesn't matter whether the subjects of desensitization and conditioning are soldiers taking target practice at a range or kids using point-and-shoot video games; the result is the same: the creation of a killing machine.

But you don't need to read Grossman's book to see the parallels he made. Young people today are exposed to violent images that desensitize them and make it possible for some of them to act out those violent images in real life. And video games help them hone their shooting skills and overcome their hesitation to kill. Dave Grossman has seen it in war, and now he is seeing it in everyday life.

Violence and Teenage Rebellion

So much has been said recently about school shootings that it's often difficult to hear solid commentary in the midst of the cacophony. But one voice deserves a hearing: Jonathan Cohen wrote a commentary titled "Defining Rebellion Up," which appeared in the *New York Post.* [3]

As background, years ago, Senator Daniel Patrick Moynihan wrote a seminal piece titled "Defining Deviancy Down," which appeared in an academic journal.[4] His contention was that in the midst of cultural chaos we tend to redefine what is normal. When the crime rate goes through the roof, we say that crime is inevitable in a free society. When the illegitimate birth rate quadruples, we say that maybe two parents in a home aren't really necessary after all. In essence, society is following the pattern in Isaiah 5:20—calling evil good and good evil.

Cohen picked up on Moynihan's theme and extended it to our current subject. He says that when America became willing to define deviancy down, it simultaneously defined rebellion up. He says, "Anti-social teens are nothing new, but as deviancy has been made normal, we have made it increasingly difficult for teenagers to rebel."

Adults are no longer offended or outraged by behavior that would have sent our parents through the roof. We have learned the lessons of tolerance perhaps too well. We tolerate just about everything from tattoos to black nail polish to metal-pierced eyebrows.

Cohen said, "We have raised the threshold of rebellion so high that it is practically beyond reach. To be recognized, to get attention, to stir anyone in authority to lift a finger, whether it is a parent, a teacher, a principal, or a sheriff, a rebel has to go to very great lengths these days. One must send letter bombs, blow up office buildings or gun down children."

If a young person is trying to defy authority, it takes quite a bit to get noticed. Just a few decades ago, when dress codes were still in effect, a student could be some-what rebellious without getting into too much trouble or hurting other people. Today, a teen must do something utterly outrageous to run afoul of those in authority.

Cohen asked, "And what of the teachers at Columbine High? It seemed they were not disturbed at all by the boys' odd conduct. In fact, one instructor actually helped them make a video dramatizing their death-and-destruction fantasy. For all we know, he may well have commended himself for being so nonjudgmental."

Cohen's last statement above raises an important point. The highest value in our society today has become toler-ance. We are not to judge others. When you combine this trend of rising rebellion with increased tolerance, you end up with a lethal mixture.

Cohen concluded by wondering if the end in Colum-bine might have been avoided. He says, "If teachers had forbidden their students from coming to class wearing black trench coats, fingernail polish and makeup, Littleton likely would not be a name on everyone's lips. If the prin-cipal had had the common sense to ban a group of boys from coming to school sporting Nazi regalia, marching though the corridors in military fashion and calling them-selves the Trench Coat Mafia, Columbine High School might not be behind a police line."

Tolerance

Because tolerance has so high a value in our society, we may miss the signals that something is wrong with our kids. After the school shooting in Colorado, an editorial titled "Too Much Tolerance?" appeared in the *New York Post.*[5] The editorial writers said, "The Littleton massacre could prove a turning point in American society—one of those moments when the entire culture changes course." The editorial writers believe that one of the things that must change is our contemporary view of tolerance.

While other pundits focused on guns, video games, and other cultural phenomena, these editorial writers said that the real cause was "inattention." The killers in Colorado were sending out signals of an impending calamity, but no one was paying attention. One Littleton parent, for example, went to the police twice about threats made by Eric Harris on his son's life. His pleas were to no avail; the cops didn't pay attention.

These kids in the Trench Coat Mafia gave each other Hitler salutes at a local bowling alley. But the community didn't pay attention.

These same kids marched down the hallways and got into fights with jocks and other kids after school. But the school didn't pay attention.

One kid's mother works with disabled kids but seemed unaware that her own son had a fascination with Adolf Hitler and spent a year planning the destruction of the high school. Again, parents didn't pay attention.

Throughout the article, the editorial writers recount all of the things that these kids did. They conclude that while they "were doing everything they could to offend the community they lived in, the community chose to pay them no heed."

Why? This tragic lack of attention is the sorry harvest of the tolerance and diversity that are preached in the nation's classrooms every day. We are not to judge others. The only sin in society is the sin of judgmentalism. We cannot judge hairstyles or lifestyles, manners or morals. We might think another person's dress, actions, or lifestyles are a bit different, but we are told not to judge. Everything must be tolerated. And so we decide to ignore in the name of tolerance.

In earlier decades, society had boundaries, school dress codes were enforced, and certain behavior was not allowed. As the boundaries were expanded and the lines of acceptable behavior became blurred, teachers and parents learned to cope by paying less attention.

The *New York Post* editorial writers conclude, "The only way Americans can live like this is to tune out, to ignore, to refuse to pay attention. In the name of broadmindedness, Littleton allowed Harris and Klebold to fall through the cracks straight to Hell."

So why do we have kids killing kids? A lot of reasons can be cited: the moral breakdown of society, video games, rebellion. But another reason is tolerance. We have been taught for decades not to judge, and this has given adults a license to be inattentive.

Spiritual Implications

Former Secretary of Education Bill Bennett appeared as a guest on one of the talking-head shows, discussing the tragedy in Littleton, Colorado. All of a sudden, he turned directly to the television camera and said, "Hello?"

That was the attention getter. But what he said afterward should also get our attention. He pointed out that these kids were walking the halls in trench coats, and apparently that didn't really get the attention of the teachers and administrators. But, he said, if a kid walked the halls with a Bible, that would probably get their attention. Something is very wrong with a society and a school system that would admonish a schoolkid for carrying a Bible and spreading the Good News while ignoring a group of kids wearing trench coats and spreading hatred.

In her *Wall Street Journal* column, former presidential speechwriter Peggy Noonan wrote about "The Culture of Death" in which our children live.[6] She quoted headlines from news stories, and frankly I can't even repeat what she quoted. Our kids are up to their necks in really awful stuff, and it comes to them day after day on television, in the movies, and in the newspapers.

Noonan then asked, "Who counters this culture of death?" Parents do and churches do, but parenting and religion has lost much of their potency in modern society. Noonan told the following story to illustrate her point:

"A man called into Christian radio this morning and said a true thing. He said, and I am paraphrasing: 'Those kids were sick and sad, and if a teacher had talked to one of them and said, "Listen, there's a way out, there really is love out there that will never stop loving you, there's a real God and I want to be able to talk to you about him"— if that teacher had intervened that way, he would have been hauled into court.'"

The man who called that radio station is right. A few years ago, a very famous case made its way through the Colorado courts. A high school teacher in Colorado was taken to court merely because he had a Bible on his desk. The conclusion won't surprise you. The teacher lost the original case and then lost again on appeal.

In addressing the disturbing phenomenon of kids killing kids, this chapter has discussed the breakdown of society, the influence of video games, rebellion, and tolerance. But the increase in youth violence contains a spiritual dimension. We are reaping the harvest of a secular society.

Kids kill other kids, and we wonder why. We throw God out of the classroom, we throw the Bible out of the classroom, we throw prayer out of the classroom, and we even throw the Ten Commandments out of the classroom.

Maybe we should no longer wonder why. Maybe we should be surprised that society isn't *more* barbaric, given that so many positive, spiritual influences have been thrown out. The ultimate solution to the problem of kids killing kids is for the nation to return to God.

Endnotes

Foreword: What Shall the Righteous Do?

1. Peter Kreeft, *Everything You Ever Wanted to Know About Heaven* (San Francisco: Ignatius Press, 1997).

Chapter 1: Technological Challenges of the Twenty-first Century

1. Memo from Charles H. Duell, Director of the U.S. Patent Office, 1899.
2. Jacques Ellul, *The Technological Society* (New York: Vintage, 1964).
3. C. S. Lewis, *The Abolition of Man* (New York: Macmillan, 1947), 68–69, 71 (italics his).
4. Ethan Singer, cited in Nicholas Wade, "Gene Splicing: Congress Starts Framing Law for Research," *Science*, 1 April 1977, 39.
5. Michael Crichton, *The Andromeda Strain* (New York: Dell, 1969).
6. Kenneth Woodward, "Thou Shalt Not Patent!" *Newsweek*, 29 May 1995, 68.
7. Testimony by Ethan Singer before the Subcommittee on Health and the Environment, House Committee on Interstate and Foreign Commerce, *Hearings*, 15 March 1977, 79.
8. Julian Huxley, cited in Joseph Fletcher, *The Ethics of Genetic Control* (Garden City, N.Y.: Anchor, 1974), 8.
9. Erwin Chargaff, cited in George Wald, "The Case Against Genetic Engineering," *The Sciences*, May 1976, 10.
10. Nancy McCann, "The DNA Maelstrom: Science and Industry Rewrite the Fifth Day of Creation," *Sojourners*, May 1977, 23–26.
11. Philip Elmer-Dewitt, "The Genetic Revolution," *Time*, 17 January 1994, 49.

12. Skeptics sometimes argue that fighting disease is the same as fighting God's will. Albert Camus poses this dilemma for Dr. Reux in *The Plague.* Christians should follow God's cultural mandate (Gen. 1:28) and use genetic technology to treat and cure genetic disease.

13. Sharon Begley, "Little Lamb, Who Made Thee?" *Newsweek,* 10 March 1997, 55.

14. James Bonner, quoted in *Los Angeles Times,* 17 May 1971, 1.

15. N. N. Glazer, *Hammer on the Rock: A Short Midrash Reader* (New York: Schocken, 1962), 15.

16. Philip Elmer-DeWitt, "A Birthday Party for ENIAC," *Time,* 24 February 1986, 63.

17. "Machine of the Year," *Time,* 3 January 1983, 13–24.

18. "Harper's Index," *Harper's,* October 1984, 9.

19. Ted Gest, "Who Is Watching You?" *U.S. News and World Report,* 12 July 1982, 35.

20. David Burnham, *The Rise of the Computer State* (New York: Random House, 1983).

21. Martha Farnsworth Riche, "The Rising Tide of Privacy Laws," *American Demographics,* March 1990, 24.

22. Richard Lipkin, "Making Machines in Mind's Image," *Insight,* 15 February 1988, 8–12.

23. Robert Mueller and Erik Mueller, "Would an Intelligent Computer Have a 'Right to Life'?" *Creative Computing,* August 1983, 149–61.

24. Danny Hillis, "Can They Feel Your Pain?" *Newsweek,* 5 May 1997, 57.

25. Robert Jastrow, "Toward an Intelligence Beyond Man's," *Time,* 20 February 1978, 59.

Chapter 2: The Value of the Internet for Christians

1. For example, Cable News Network's home page is www.cnn.com. You can also check the Web sites of newspapers and TV networks and stations.

2. Use a search engine with the keywords "+speech+RealAudio" to see a list of speeches online.

3. Music is such a broad category that your best bet is to use a search engine (see note 16) to find sites that offer the kind of music you would like to hear, such as "Country Music" or "Gospel Music" or "Japanese Music."

4. The Internet is a mind-boggling collection of information, and search engines—like instant electronic librarians—are the best way to find information about whatever subject in which you're interested. (See note 11.)

5. These "library malls" are analogous to FTP (File Transfer Protocol) sites.

6. The "conversation malls" are analogous to IRC (Internet Relay Channels) rooms, as well as the immensely popular chat rooms now available on the World Wide Web. You can find thousands of them by going to any search engine and typing in "chat rooms" as the keywords. Be forewarned, however, that these rooms can be dangerous places for children, and I suggest that people stay out of them.

7. You can get information about this list and others like it by using search engines. For instance, use "brain tumor list" as the keywords to get information on all the lists available for this particular subject.

8. NASA's home page is http://www.nasa.gov/NASA_homepage.html. The *Houston Chronicle* offers an exceptional Web page on which you can see various space-related photos and even listen to shuttle launchings and landings, as well as live transmissions when the shuttle is on a mission. Find it at http://www.chron.com/content/interactive/space and click on "NASA TV Video." Another good route is to go to Yahoo (see note 11) and look in the index under "Hobbies, Astronomy."

9. You can get either comprehensive or free, but not both. Britannica Online (www.eb.com) is comprehensive, but you have to pay a monthly fee to access it. The free encyclopedias are not comprehensive; one place to find some is at www.yahoo.com/Reference/Encyclopedia/.

10. The online services are probably the best sources for libraries (files contributed by members). One particularly good online community that includes a library is the Home School forum on CompuServe's Christian Interactive Network. You no longer need a CompuServe membership to access this site: go.compuserve.com/cinhomesch.

11. Several search engines are available on the Internet, all of which are free. My personal favorite is Google, http://www.google.com. Some others to try include the following:
    Altavista: http://www.altavista.com
    Yahoo: http://www.yahoo.com
    Lycos: http://www.lycos.com
    Go.com: http://www.go.com
    Ask Jeeves: http://www.askjeeves.com
    I avoid Metacrawler (www.metacrawler.com) because pornographic ads can appear on its results pages.

12. www.probe.org/docs/angels.html.

13. iclnet93.iclnet.org/pub/resources/christian-books.html.

14. iclnet93.iclnet.org/pub/resources/christian-history.html.

15. www.citilink.com/~dsands/midi.html.
16. Quentin Schultze, *Internet for Christians* (Muskegon, Mich.: Gospel Films, 1998).
17. Jason Baker, *Parents' Computer Companion* (Grand Rapids: Baker, 1999).

Chapter 3: Protecting Your Family on the Internet

1. "The NetValue Report on Minors Online," *Business Wire,* 19 December 2000.
2. I recommend two Web sites for people addicted to porn and those who love them. The first is divided into two sections, one for addicts and one for family and friends, http://www.pureintimacyorg. The other is www.settingcaptivesfree.com, which features an online Bible study program through which many have found freedom.
3. http://www.protectkids.com/.
4. http://www.ozarkcountry.com/jerry.
5. The Kim Komando National Talkradio Show E-Zine, 26 May 2001.
6. http://www.natlconsumersleague.org/susantestimony52301.html.
7. http://www.fraud.org/scamsagainstbusinesses/tips/nigerian.htm.

Chapter 4: Cyberporn

1. Philip Elmer-DeWitt, "On a Screen Near You: Cyberporn," *Time,* 3 July 1995, 40.
2. Steven Levy, "No Place for Kids?" *Newsweek,* 3 July 1995, 48.
3. G. A. Servi, "Sexy F Seeks Hot M: A Mother's Tale," *Newsweek,* 3 July 1995, 51.
4. Elmer-DeWitt, "On a Screen Near You: Cyberporn," 38–40.
5. Ibid., 42.
6. Brad Store, "Low-Tech Parents Aren't Powerless," *Newsweek,* 3 July 1995, 50.
4. Joshua Quittner, "How Parents Can Filter Out the Naughty Bits," *Time,* 3 July 1995, 45.

Chapter 5: Privacy Issues

1. Ron Paul, "Legislation Brought Forward to Stop National ID," press release from Congressman Ron Paul's office, 15 July 1998.
2. Ibid.
3. Bob Barr, "Don't Give Washington Bureaucrats the Tool to Track Us from Cradle to Grave," *Insight,* 24 August 1998, 25.
4. Paul Wiseman, "Lifetime Medical ID Number Being Considered," *USA Today,* 21 July 1998, 9A.
5. Ibid.

6. "Restriction on Export of U.S. Encryption Products Are Futile at Best," Cato News Release, 12 November 1998.
7. Brian Clark, "Indecent Exposure," *Money.Com,* Special Issue (fall 1998): 78.
8. Ibid., 80.

Chapter 6: Online Affairs
1. Peggy Vaughn, *The Monogamy Myth* (New York: Newmarket, 1998).
2. Karen Peterson, "Spouses Browse Infidelity Online," *USA Today,* 6 July 1999, 1D.
3. Kerby Anderson, ed., *Marriage, Family, and Sexuality* (Grand Rapids: Kregel, 2000).
4. Philip Blumstein and Pepper Schwartz, *American Couples* (New York: William Morrow, 1983).
5. Maggie Scarf, *Intimate Partners* (New York: Ballantine, 1996).
6. Trish Hall, "Infidelity and Women: Shifting Patterns," *New York Times,* 1 June 1987, B8.
7. Annette Lawson, *Adultery: An Analysis of Love and Betrayal* (New York: Basic Books,1988).
8. Alfred Kinsey, et al., *Sexual Behavior in the Human Female* (Philadelphia: W. B. Saunders, 1953).
9. R. Athanasiou, et al., "Sex: A Report to *Psychology Today* Readers," *Psychology Today,* July 1970, 39–52.
10. Shere Hite, *Women and Love* (New York: Alfred Knopf, 1987).
11. Carol Travis and Susan Sadd, *The Redbook Report on Female Sexuality* (New York: Delacorte Press, 1977).
12. "Infidelity Survey," *New Woman,* October–November 1986.
13. Linda Wolfe, *Playing Around: Women and Extramarital Sex* (New York: William Morrow, 1975).
14. Frank Pittman, *Private Lies: Infidelity and the Betrayal of Intimacy* (New York: Norton, 1989).
15. Jan Halper, *Quiet Desperation: The Truth About Successful Men* (New York: Warner Books, 1988).
16. William Allman, "The Mating Game," *U.S. News and World Report,* 19 July 1993, 57–63.

Chapter 7: Human Cloning
1. Ray Bohlin, "Can Humans Be Cloned Like Sheep?" *Probe Perspective* (1997).
2. Vittorio Sgaramella and Norton D. Zinder, "Letters," *Science* 279 (30 January 1998): 635–36.

3. J. Madeleine Nash, "Was Dolly a Mistake?" *Time,* 2 March 1998, 65.
4. D. Ashworth, et al., "DNA Microsatellite Analysis of Dolly," *Nature* 394 (23 July 1998): 329; and E. Signer, et al., "DNA Fingerprinting Dolly" *Nature* 394 (23 July 1998): 329–30.
5. Davor Soltor, "Dolly Is a Clone—and No Longer Alone," *Nature* 394 (23 July 1998): 315–16.
6. T. Wakayama, et al., "Full-term Development of Mice from Enucleated Oocytes Injected with Cumulus Cell Nuclei," *Nature* 394 (23 July 1998): 369–74.
7. Rachel K. Sobel, "Copying a Multitude of Mice: Cloning Is No Fluke; Wooly Mammoths Next?" *U.S. News and World Report,* 3 August 1998, 52.
8. Ian Wilmut, "Cloning for Medicine," *Scientific American* 279.6 (December 1998): 58–63.
9. James A. Thomason, et al., "Embryonic Stem Cell Lines Derived from Human Blastocysts," *Science* 282 (6 November 1998): 1145–47.
10. Declan Butler, "Breakthrough Stirs US Embryo Debate," *Nature* 396 (12 November 1998): 104.
11. Ibid.
12. Wesley J. Smith, "The Politics of Stem Cells," *The Weekly Standard,* 26 March 2001, 17–20.
13. Richard Seed, quoted on the Fox News Channel program, *Trends,* 8 December 1997.
14. http://www.boston.com/dailynews/wirehtml/250/Chicago_physicist_says_he_ll_clone_.shtml. 9/8/98.
15. Richard Seed, quoted on *ABC News Nightline,* 7 January 1998.
16. John Pickerell, "Experts Assail Plan to Help Childless Couples," *Science* 291 (16 March 2001): 2061–63.
17. Nancy Gibbs, "Baby, It's You! And You. And You . . . ," *Time,* 19 February 2001, 55.
18. Pickerell, "Experts Assail Plan to Help Childless Couples," 2061–63.
19. Ellen Goodman, "Clone Con Job," *The Dallas Morning News,* 4 April 2001, 15A.
20. Gibbs, "Baby, It's You! And You. And You . . . ," 57.
21. James Robl, quoted in *The Cloning Revolution,* films for the Humanities and Sciences (1998), P.O. Box 2053, Princeton, NJ 08543-2053.

Chapter 8: Human Genome Project

1. "Genetics: The Future of Medicine," *National Institutes of Health,* publication no. 00–4873, 2.

2. *Nature* 409 (15 February 2001), www.nature.com.
3. *Science* 291 (16 February 2001), www.sciencemag.org.
4. "Genetics: The Future of Medicine," 9–11.
5. Kevin Davies, "After the Genome: DNA and Human Disease," *Cell* 104 (23 February 2001): 465–67.
6. http://www.probe.org/docs/e-genome.html.
7. Wen-Siung Li, Zhenglong Gu, Haidong Waing, and Anton Nekrutenko, "Evolutionary Analyses of the Human Genome," *Nature* 409 (15 February 2001): 847–49.
8. Tom Abate, "Human Genome Map Has Scientists Talking About the Divine—Surprisingly low number of genes raises big questions," *San Francisco Chronicle*, 19 February 2001.
9. James M. Jeffords and Tom Daschle, "Political Issues in the Genomic Era," *Science* 291 (16 February 2001) 1249–51.
10. For a fictional, yet intelligent, exploration of this possibility, see the 1997 science fiction film *Gattaca*.

Chapter 9: Baby Boomerangs

1. Information in this chapter taken from Kerby Anderson's book *Signs of Warning, Signs of Hope* (Chicago: Moody, 1994).
2. George Johnston, "Break Glass in Case of Emergency," *Beyond the Boom*, ed. Terry Teachout (New York: Poseidon, 1990), 55.
3. Faith Popcorn, *Adweek's Marketing Week*, 18 May 1987, 12.
4. Ken Sidey, "A Generation on the Doorstep," *Moody*, January 1987, 22.
5. Augustine, *Confessions* 1.1.
6. Ken Woodword, "A Time to Seek," *Newsweek*, 17 December 1990, 51.
7. George Gallup and Jim Castells, *The People's Religion* (New York: Macmillan, 1989), 132–48.
8. Wesley Pippert, "A Generation Warms to Religion," *Christianity Today*, 6 October 1989, 22.
9. Ibid.
10. Ibid., 23.
11. Johnston, "Break Glass," 59.
12. "Fewer than 10% of Americans Are Deeply Committed Christians," *National and International Religion Report*, 20 May 1991, 1.
13. Ibid.
14. "Gallup Tells Editors: Americans Revere the Bible, Don't Read It," *World*, 19 May 1990, 8.

Chapter 10: Generation X

1. William Dunn, *The Baby Bust: A Generation Comes of Age* (Ithaca, N.Y.: American Demographics Books, 1993), 112.
2. Quentin J. Schultze, ed., *Dancing in the Dark: Youth, Popular Culture, and the Electronic Media* (Grand Rapids, Mich.: Eerdmans, 1991), 14.
3. Ibid., 19.
4. Steven J. Novak, *The Rights of Youth: American Colleges and Student Revolt, 1798–1815* (Cambridge, Mass.: Harvard, 1977), 17–25. Quoted in Schultze, *Dancing in the Dark,* 23.
5. Schultze, *Dancing in the Dark,* 33.
6. Joseph F. Kett, *Rites of Passage: Adolescence in America, 1790 to the Present* (New York: Basic Books, 1977), 243. Quoted in Schultze, *Dancing in the Dark,* 35.
7. Schultze, *Dancing in the Dark,* 35.
8. Ibid., 45.
9. George Barna, *Generation Next: What You Need to Know About Today's Youth* (Ventura, Calif.: Regal, 1995), 11.
10. Dunn, *Baby Bust,* x.
11. Barna, *Generation Next,* 18.
12. Dunn, *Baby Bust,* x.
13. Ibid., 16.
14. Barna, *Generation Next,* 18–21.
15. Jan Johnson, "Getting the Gospel to the Baby Busters," *Moody Monthly,* May 1995, 50.
16. Ibid.
17. Ibid., 51.
18. Barna, *Generation Next,* 108–15.
19. Jay Kesler, *Ten Mistakes Parents Make with Teenagers (And How to Avoid Them)* (Brentwood, Tenn.: Wolgemuth & Hyatt, 1988).

Chapter 11: The Spiritual Quest of Generation X

1. Joan Osborne, "One of Us," on the album *Relish,* Uni/Mercury, 1995. Downloaded from http://lyrics.astraweb.com:2000/display.cgi?joan_osborne%2E%2Erelish%2E%2Eone_of_us, 17 February 2001.
2. Tom Beaudoin, *Virtual Faith: The Irreverent Spiritual Question of Generation X* (San Francisco: Jossey-Bass, 1998), 53.
3. Cf. ibid., 74–75.
4. Ibid., xiii–xiv.
5. Jimmy Long, *Generating Hope: A Strategy for Reaching the Postmodern Generation* (Downers Grove, Ill.: InterVarsity, 1997), 43.

6. See Jerry Solomon, "Generation X," an overview of this generation, available on our Web site at www.probe.org/docs/genera-x.html.
7. Long, *Generating Hope*, 48, quoting Andrew Smith, "Talking About My Generation," *The Face*, July 1994, 82.
8. Tim Celek and Dieter Zander, *Inside the Soul of a New Generation: Insights and Strategies for Reaching Busters* (Grand Rapids: Zondervan, 1996), 46.
9. Ibid., 51.
10. Ibid., 31–32.
11. Douglas Coupland, *Life After God* (New York: Pocket Books, 1994), 273.
12. Ibid., 310, 313, 359.
13. Osborne, "One of Us."
14. David Hocking, *The Nature of God in Plain Language* (Waco, Tex.: Word, 1984), 65.
15. Coupland, *Life After God*, 359.
16. Celek and Zander, *Inside the Soul*, 55.
17. Hocking, *Nature of God*, 145. I am indebted to the author for the outline of this section.

Chapter 12: Time and Busyness

1. Nancy Gibbs, "How America Has Run Out of Time," *Time*, 24 April 1989, 58.
2. Ibid.
3. Laurence Shames, *The Hunger for More* (New York: Times Books, 1989), 59.
4. Ibid.
5. Ibid.
6. Leslie Barker, "We Never Seem to Talk Any More," *Dallas Morning News*, 25 September 1989, C1.
7. Ibid.
8. Gibbs, "Out of Time," 58.
9. David Elkin, *The Hurried Child* (Reading, Mass.: Addison-Wesley, 1981).
10. Stephanie Abarbanel and Karen Peterson, "Never Enough Time? You Can Beat the Clock," *Family Circle*, 14 March 1989, 115.
11. Ibid., 116.
12. Ibid.
13. Ibid., 119.
14. Ibid., 136.

Chapter 13: Loneliness

1. Martha Farnsworth Riche, "The Postmarital Society," *American Demographics,* November 1988, 24.
2. Landon Jones, *Great Expectations* (New York: Ballantine, 1980), 215.
3. Thomas Exeter, "Alone at Home," *American Demographics,* April 1990, 55.
4. Dan Kiley, *Living Together, Feeling Alone* (New York: Prentice-Hall, 1989).
5. Dixie Reed, "Alone Together," *Dallas Times Herald,* 20 November 1989, B1, 3.
6. Herb Goldberg, *The Hazards of Being Male* (New York: New American Library, 1976).
7. David Smith, *Men Without Friends* (Nashville: Nelson, 1990), 24–30.
8. H. Norman Wright, *Seasons of a Marriage* (Ventura, Calif.: Regal, 1982), 75.
9. Quoted in Dennis Rainey, *Lonely Husbands, Lonely Wives* (Dallas: Word, 1989), 11–12.
10. Ralph Keyes, *We the Lonely People: Searching for Community* (New York: HarperCollins, 1973).
11. Vance Packard, *A Nation of Strangers* (New York: David McKay, 1972), 2–5.

Chapter 14: Midlife Transition

1. Cartoon reprinted in article by Daniel B. Moskowitz, "The Trappings of Success—Or Just a Trap?" *Business Week,* 6 February 1989.
2. Daniel Levinson, *The Seasons of a Man's Life* (New York, Knopf, 1978).
3. Gail Sheehy, *Passages: Predictable Crisis of Adult Life* (New York: Bantam, 1974).
4. "Aging of a Yuppie, the Making of MOSS," *Dallas Times Herald,* 15 June 1989, E1.
5. Ibid.
6. Levinson, *Seasons of a Man's Life,* ix.
7. Ibid., 28.
8. Ibid.
9. Ibid., 215.

Chapter 15: Sex and Violence on Television

1. Parents Television Council, *Special Report: What a Difference a Decade Makes,* 30 March 2000. For full report see the Web site (www.parentstv.org).
2. David Grossman, "What the Surgeon General Found: As Early as

1972, the Link Was Clear Between Violent TV and Movies and Violent Youths," *Los Angeles Times,* 21 October 1999, B11.

3. See Parents Television Council, *Special Report: The Family Hour: Worse Than Ever and Headed for New Lows,* 30 August 1999.

4. Veronis, Suhler & Associates, Wilkofsky Gruen Associates, from Television Bureau of Advertising, Consumer Media Usage, TV Basics (www.tvb.org/tvfacts/tvbasics27.htm).

5. *National Family Values: A Survey of Adults* conducted by Voter/Consumer Research (Bethesda, Md., 1994).

6. See the article, "Pornography," available at the Probe Web site (www.probe.org).

7. Neil Malamuth and Edward Donnerstein, *Pornography and Sexual Aggression* (New York: Academic, 1984).

8. Edward Donnerstein, "What the Experts Say," a forum at the Industry-wide Leadership Conference on Violence in Television Programming, 2 August 1993, in *National Council for Families and Television Report,* 9.

9. Irving Kristol, "Sex, Violence, and Videotape," *Wall Street Journal,* 31 May 1994.

10. John Johnston, "Kids: Growing Up Scared," *Cincinnati Enquirer,* 20 March 1994, E01.

11. Cited in "Warning from Washington," *Time,* 17 May 1982, 77.

12. James Mann, "What Is TV Doing to America?" *U.S. News and World Report,* 2 August 1982, 27.

13. Leo Bogart, "Warning: The Surgeon General Has Determined That TV Violence Is Moderately Dangerous to Your Child's Mental Health," *Public Opinion,* winter 1972–73, 504.

14. Peter Plagen, "Violence in Our Culture," *Newsweek,* 1 April 1991, 51.

15. Ibid.

16. George Gerbner and Larry Gross, "The Scary World of TV's Heavy Viewer," *Psychology Today,* April 1976.

17. Ibid.

18. Ibid.

Chapter 16: Kids Killing Kids

1. Andrea Billups and Jerry Seper, "Experts Hit Permissiveness in Schools, Violence on TV," *The Washington Times,* 22 April 1999.

2. Dave Grossman, *On Killing: The Psychological Cost of Learning to Kill in War and Society* (New York: Little, Brown, 1996).

3. Jonathan Cohen, "Defining Rebellion Up," *New York Post,* 27 April 1999.

4. Daniel Patrick Moynihan, "Defining Deviancy Down," *The American Spectator,* winter 1993.

5. "Too Much Tolerance?" *New York Post,* 27 April 1999.
6. Peggy Noonan, "The Culture of Death," *Wall Street Journal,* 22 April 1999.